LIVING THREADS

Making the Quaker Tapestry

Jennie Levin

ISBN 0 9525433 3 8

Designed by Jeremy Greenwood, Woodbridge
and printed by Middletons of Ambleside
Compston Road, Ambleside, Cumbria LA22 9DJ

for The Quaker Tapestry at Kendal
Friends Meeting House, Stramongate
Kendal, Cumbria LA9 4BH

the permanent home of the
Quaker Tapestry Collection

Table of contents

'The chief attribute of a good embroiderer is love'
Anne Wynn-Wilson

Living Threads is dedicated to Anne Wynn-Wilson, founder of the Quaker Tapestry, who died suddenly on 13 October 1998, aged 72. It was her vision, inspiration, devotion, and generosity in giving 15 years of her life to travelling in the ministry with this work that made it possible for thousands of others to contribute to it, enjoy it and learn from it. Thank you Anne.

This book and its associated research were commissioned by the Quaker Tapestry Publications Committee, which I thank for giving me both the most difficult and most rewarding job of my life. What I learned from it is that a true community is a group of people with a shared aim and with powerful commitments both to fulfilling that aim and to ensuring that any difficulties that stand in the way of doing so are resolved or overcome. I do not know how far Anne Wynn-Wilson's original aims of promoting community, education and opportunity within the Religious Society of Friends as a whole have been fulfilled, but am quite clear that a strong sense of community developed among those committed to working with the Quaker Tapestry. It was this that made the scheme work and it continues to flourish, inspiring more people to become involved in exhibitions and outreach.

My sources for the text are embroidery groups' written accounts of making panels, other written sources, including Anne Wynn-Wilson's original proposals and the Constitution of the Quaker Tapestry Scheme, a series of tape recordings made for the Quaker Tapestry archives with groups and individuals who took part in the scheme, minutes of meetings of the QTS committee and some of its sub-committees, *Quaker Tapestry newsletters*, and personal conversations and correspondence.

Hundreds of people have contributed to my work, some of whom have generously given a great deal of time and expertise. I give particular thanks to: Anne Wynn-Wilson, Ann Castle, Ann Nichols, Margaret Simpson, Kathleen Cottrell, Jeremy Greenwood, Bridget Guest, Betty Harris, Daniel Keeler, Edward Milligan, and Renate Warner. The text would never have been completed without the love, practical help and encouragement of these Friends, my partner David Geach, his sister Ann Lavers, and my dear friends Betty Calderwood and Kate Sykes.

I have endeavoured to give as truthful an overall picture of the making of the tapestry as I can, though people's experiences were so varied that my interpretation could not encompass them all. In any case, different people see the same events in different ways. I share the sorrow of those whose panels or other contributions are not included and apologise for any mistakes or misunderstandings.

Jennie Levin, November 1998

ILLUSTRATION ACKNOWLEDGMENTS

Brian Boothby: p. 32 (left).
Bridget Guest: pp. 61 (left), 62.
Grace Johannsen: p. 41.
Jennie Levin: pp. 10, 14 (both), 17, 18, 26, 31, 33, 52, 54, 57 (both).
Ann Nichols: p. 27.
Sacha Playfair: p. 30.
Janet Sewell: p. 44.
Margaret Simpson: pp. 48 (left), 56.
Anne Wynn-Wilson: pp. 11, 13 (right), 22, 36, 39, 50, 51. Ann Wynn-Wilson's collection: pp. 13 (left), 16, 21, 28, 30, 50, 58, 61 (right).
Bryn Lennon Photography: front and back covers, pp. 7, 9, 23, 38 (right), 42 (all three), 47.
The Leaveners: p. 37.
Long Ashton Research Station: p. 15.
Scottish Tapestry group: p. 46.
Mid-Somerset monthly meeting group: p. 38 (left).
New Zealand Friends: p. 49.
North American Quaker Tapestry: p. 48 (right).
Ville de Bayeux: p. 8.
The line drawings throughout the text are taken from designs for Tapestry panels.

Introduction

The Quaker Tapestry is a celebration of more than 300 years of Quaker insights and experiences embroidered in narrative crewel work on 77 panels of specially woven wool cloth. Each panel measures 25 in. × 21 in. It could also be seen as a celebration of the imagination, craftsmanship, tenacity and determination of the Quakers of the late twentieth century who made it.

The scheme that evolved to design, oversee and develop the embroidery project was for tapestry founder Anne Wynn-Wilson the point of the exercise. Embroidery was the medium that provided the opportunities for what she describes as an experiment in education, communication and community experience.

Its underlying aims are perhaps best described in Anne's own words: 'I sensed within the (Religious) Society (of Friends) pockets of loneliness, especially among the elderly, and a lack of knowledge about Quaker experience amongst newcomers and children. Because the tapestry had not been commissioned, I was free to base the project on people, their needs and well-being . . . I wanted to give people opportunities, to see a problem, to work out how to solve it, and to encourage sharing and interdependence. So it was very important to create a style and technique that could be enjoyed both by experienced embroiderers and by the young or unskilled.'

The scheme was, indeed, to offer all this. Some 4,000 people in 15 countries, many completely without experience of embroidery, were enabled to put in at least a stitch or two by the 300 or so embroiderers who carried out the main part of the

work. Others broadened their horizons in unexpected ways as research led them to investigate subjects as diverse as sixteenth-century trade and the texture of ermine. Problems to be solved ranged from how to embroider convincing looking chains and ropes (solutions on different panels were macramé chains and the use of a food mixer to twist wools into rope) to delving into records to discover what people looked like, how they dressed and how their ships were rigged.

As might be expected in a project of this size, some groups fostered community in the way that they organised their work, others found that very difficult. Some individuals travelled countries, continents or widely within their own locality with panels, others worked alone in their homes. Many made deep and lasting friendships and learned new and exciting skills.

The scheme gathered a momentum of its own as it moved from the research, design and embroidery stage to the exhibition stage. Many of its educational, communication and community possibilities remain to be explored. Some 300 people are now involved in the permanent tapestry exhibition at Kendal and in working with the small travelling exhibitions, publications and market,

their voluntary work ranging from stewarding to packaging, from accountancy to gardening.

This book distils some of the experiences of Friends over the first 15 years of the Quaker Tapestry Scheme. It seeks to give readers an insight into what the scheme has been like for those taking part and how they have managed to overcome the many difficulties involved in maintaining the high standard of work expected of them.

In some ways the design of the book resembles the design of a tapestry panel. Mountains of research were mined for gems of individual experience, each of which could provide insights into the whole. The stories of a few must capture the essence of the experience of all those involved.

The tapestry scheme was of its time. The second half of the twentieth century saw a great flowering of community projects of all kinds, especially in the decorative arts and crafts. Community embroideries hang in town halls, churches and exhibitions across the country and across the world. But the Quaker Tapestry is quite unlike any other contemporary embroidery in its style, scope, content, method of execution and consequent effect on many of those who took part.

In hearing the stories of people who worked on the tapestry I am constantly reminded both of the ways in which the tapestry is unique and of the way in which it is part of a long tradition of art for the glory of God that stretches back into the mists of history. It was conceived out of a living faith, illuminates key aspects of that faith, was embroidered in faith, is exhibited in faith and is known to have affected some individuals' spiritual journeys.

Yet while the Quaker Tapestry may be seen as resting firmly in the tradition of art for the glory of God, it is a novel venture for Quakers, whose meeting places, homes and persons have traditionally been plain. In the eighteenth and nineteenth centuries all the decorative arts and crafts were frowned upon, with fashionable dress and theatre singled out as particular abominations.

Changes in attitude in the twentieth century are reflected in the subjects of some of the tapestry panels, such as *Quaker Peace Action Caravan*, B8, and *Leaveners*, C11, both theatre-based, and in Friends' rejection of uniform plain dress. Today's Friends see no contradiction in appreciating beauty and leading a life of simplicity, though their faith is still deeply rooted in the religious heritage that is celebrated in the tapestry.

A brief history and description of the Religious Society of Friends is included in the appendix on page 63. The appendix on page 64 lists the panels and indicates how they were classified.

A vision of community

'I haven't never NOT seen a purple fish,' said young Ben, clutching purple and mauve wools and looking his teacher firmly in the eye with all the determination a seven-year-old spokesman for his tribe could muster.

The other children watched silently.

Their teacher, reflecting on the perils of offering free choice, threaded a needle for the first of the eight or so children to embroider purple fishes on the *Voyage of the Woodhouse* panel of the Quaker Tapestry, eyed her jumbled work box where 120 skeins of different coloured wools had once been laid out in neat rows, and wondered why she, an experienced teacher, had ever allowed herself to get into this situation.

When the children had finished their painstaking work she knew. They were right. Her work box would never be quite the same again, but the rather dull fish she had envisaged would have been insignificant while the children's purple fish are one of the glories of the very beautiful embroidery made by Nottingham meeting.

Far to the north, an Orkney farmer's wife pushed open her kitchen door on a dark, rainy, windy February evening. The phone was ringing. 'I had just sat on the buckrake of a tractor for a mile across the fields holding a ewe that had been stuck on her back in a dip with one eye picked out by

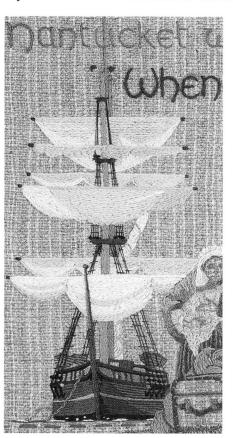

The Nantucket whaler on panel F12, embroidered by a member of Milford Haven group.

crows. I was soaking, extremely smelly and concerned about the sheep.

'The news that two Friends were thinking of visiting Orkney with the Quaker Tapestry was almost as good as the visit itself. The phone call seemed to come from another world, one of order and creative leisure. Afterwards I wondered if I might have gone over the top with my enthusiastic response and frightened them away.'

Another Scottish Friend tells how the tapestry brought her an adventure of a more intellectual kind: 'I went to the Scottish Record Office, a real first for me, and then had to be constantly shushed as I squealed with excitement as more and more wonderful pieces of research were uncovered in the SILENT room.

'I now also have a card for the Scottish National Library. Places such as these were hitherto totally unthought of,' she writes.

A Friend travelling with the Australian panel had a rather frightening experience: 'Some very dear friends have a cottage in the bush, some distance from Sydney. One day while I was there, my host and hostess went blackberrying and left me working on the tapestry on the veranda of this house, way out in the bush, miles from anywhere. As I was quietly stitching away I heard footsteps . . . thud . . . thud . . . thud.

Part of the opening scene of the Bayeux Tapestry, an embroidery that Anne Wynn-Wilson had studied in great detail before she was given her vision of a Quaker Tapestry.

'"My goodness, it's a tramp," I thought. "If I scream nobody will hear me. I've just got to put up with it." I got up and crept round the corner – and there was a wallaby! His leaps made so much noise on the bare earth that they really sounded like footsteps.'

For some Friends, working on a panel had deep meaning. This is the experience of a retired engineer who embroidered the Nantucket whaler on the *Nantucket and Milford Haven* panel: 'That week's work is likely to be more enduring than anything else I have ever done in my life, which is really quite surprising. In my working life I built factories all over the world that cost millions of pounds and the tapestry is a tiny little thing.

'It is obviously going to endure in time more than any of these other things. Already I know some of the factories I built have been closed and demolished. They pass, while this work we have done is enduring. I was conscious of that while I was working on it.'

More mundane, but no less exciting for the Friend concerned, was the discovery in a locked safe in her meeting house of old minute books relating to First Day Schools and Adult Schools – a pioneering adult education movement that Friends were involved in during most of the nineteenth century and into the twentieth. Some of the records had been made by her father.

Wellingborough meeting had chosen to research and embroider a panel, E7, on the adult school movement. A member of the group, recalling that local Friends had been much involved, said: 'It brought life to Friends. They enjoyed themselves. They couldn't be quite so quiet with handbell ringing, teas, social gatherings and lantern slides to keep the interest of the men and their families.'

Groups had very different experiences of working together. One group leader wrote: 'Foremost in our minds was the opportunity the panel gave us to meet, discuss, and enjoy learning together: so we wanted to work as a group, not pass the panel round for each to contribute . . . At all stages we discuss, share difficulties and successes and try to be receptive to constructive criticism. We have learned a lot from this part of the activity. . . We are enjoying our panel.'

George Fox preaching, *from panel B1, showing both simple and creative use of stitches. Compare this with the scene opposite, showing King Edward of England with his ambitious brother-in-law Harold and squire, from the Bayeux Tapestry to see how Anne Wynn-Wilson's use of modern techniques makes the Quaker Tapestry so different from the 800-year-old work.*

Another group said: 'Friends found it difficult to work as a coherent group and getting the tapestry finished was a struggle.'

Yet other Friends remember their experiences stewarding at Bayeux: 'I sit at a little table set on the red-tiled floor of the Salle des Chevaliers in Bayeux, between the twelfth-century cream stone pillars. There on the walls around me hang the Quaker Tapestry panels', wrote one.

'The visitors move slowly round, their eyes riveted on the panels. I look anxiously to see what colour leaflets they hold, white for English or blue for French. Blue. I tackle another stumbling conversation, to explain as best I can how a design is transferred to a panel for embroidery and how many stitches have to be taught to the Friends who make the embroidery.

'How attentively two elderly French ladies listen to my poor efforts. "Magnifique!" they exclaim. "Merveilleuse! C'est belle, très belle."'

Another steward was particularly struck by the contrast between the tapestry and the world outside. 'It was a very hot week. All round there were tanks and war and graveyards and landing beaches, even the Bayeux Tapestry is a history of war and invasion – and the Gulf war broke out while we were there. So many people came in and said "It's so cool here, and so peaceful,"' she said.

An entry in the visitors' book recalls this: 'War is contrary to the mind of Christ. If only everybody thought this. (Written during the Gulf crisis).'

Such stories will weave their way through the fabric of this book as the story of making the Quaker Tapestry unfolds, for this was a project that was as liberating for some twentieth-century Friends as the adult school movement was for their nineteenth-century predecessors.

For others it was just something their meeting did or, in a few cases, pressure rather than pleasure as they strove to finish panels for the big exhibitions. But these experiences seem to be in a minority. Even, and sometimes especially, where there were difficulties to be overcome, many Friends discovered resources and skills they did not know they had.

This was one of the aims of the Quaker Tapestry, which was offered to Friends in Britain at their 1982 yearly meeting, the annual business meeting of the Religious Society of Friends, by Anne Wynn-Wilson, then of Taunton meeting.

Anne, a professional embroiderer, first received the idea for the tapestry on the morning of 14 January 1981 as a vision, which she describes as complete in almost every detail.

'For many years I had practised the mental discipline which Quakers refer to as 'Standing in the Light'. The experience is closely linked in my mind with the gift of creativity.

'Peak experiences are difficult to describe in words, in my case because I often think in patterns.

'In the early days of January 1981, I felt a sense of freedom and heightened perception, and the interdependent patterns which were to become the Tapestry Project were very clear. One of these concerned the diverse needs of people; another, a large narrative crewel embroidery, linked throughout with a pattern of organisation and time. The whole was a new permutation of existing experience and I recognised its special meaning.

'The experience happened like this: on that January morning I was alone, washing up the breakfast dishes, when I saw the patterns and recognised their significance. I did not see the visions outside myself; I knew the idea inside.'

Anne remembers laughing out loud in sheer happiness and imagining the faces of Friends in her meeting when she told them of it. How could she begin to convince people that an embroidery project might be used as a means of building

Anne Wynn-Wilson with the linked drawings that suggested linked tapestry panels.

community and as a catalyst for finding enjoyable ways of studying Quaker history? It was an astonishing idea, but she knew at once that it was no idle dream. It could work and she had the technical ability to see it through.

She would devise an embroidery scheme that would be unified in its design, fabric and materials, yet diverse enough in technique and subject matter to draw together groups of people with differing interests and abilities.

Each element in the vision had contributed to showing her the way. She remembers standing quietly in case the detail should fade before she had understood it. Children and those on the fringe of their meetings represented the need for such a scheme. There were so many meetings like her own with just one or two children, or hesitant new attenders, who could so easily not be part of the main activities of the meeting. The Bayeux tapestry provided Anne with the insight that very simple stitches and techniques could provide the basis for complex and exciting pictures; while the idea of using a series of individual panels, which could be worked on simultaneously in different places, came from remembering that her daughter Jane, when a schoolgirl, once made a series of linked drawings as a Christmas present for her.

The Quaker Tapestry was to be a 'Bayeux in bits' that could offer scope for all to contribute according to their needs and abilities.

From vision to reality

Jonathan Stocks, of Taunton meeting, working on the first panel of the Quaker Tapestry.

Children were at the heart of the tapestry scheme from the very earliest days as it was a twelve-year-old boy, Jonathan Stocks, the only child of his age in Anne's Taunton meeting children's class at the time, who supplied the catalyst that brought about her vision.

The two of them had been discussing the idea of making an illustrated scroll depicting Quaker history, which would combine study with making something decorative to cheer up the walls of the rather gloomy room they had to use for their class.

Jonathan, who knew Anne was an embroiderer, suggested they might embroider their scroll . . . and found himself working with Anne on the first panel of the Quaker Tapestry.

He was young enough to accept without question that he and Anne might be developing a project much bigger than themselves – anything seems possible to a twelve-year-old. His teacher's natural ability to find ways of making learning interesting and to take children's ideas seriously made his

Quaker classes fun as well as hard work. Why shouldn't other children share his good fortune?

'The idea of a Quaker Tapestry began in 1981 in the Friends meeting house in Bath Place, Taunton, where my family were regular attenders,' he later wrote for his village's community magazine.

'More specifically it began in the room where I and my teacher, Anne Wynn-Wilson, held a children's meeting. Cold and damp, it desperately needed cheering up.

'Pictures were the obvious answer, a brief history of Quakerism perhaps? Only, pictures didn't inspire me as I had spent many Sunday mornings colouring pictures depicting bible stories in the young children's meeting.

'I suggested collage or a mosaic as a far more interesting medium. Anne was very interested in these ideas and before long we had progressed to the idea of a tapestry.

'Our enthusiasm for the idea was great and it soon became apparent that this was not just a project for the two of us. Hence the Quaker Tapestry was born.'

Jonathan began by studying *George Fox and the valiant sixty*, a history of early Quakers by Elfrida Vipont, while Anne read *The journal of George Fox*. Each week they discussed what they had learned and they gradually began to build up pictures both of Fox's struggles to make sense of his own life and of the kind of life people were leading in mid-sixteenth-century England.

At the same time, Anne was focusing on the lonely spiritual journeys that she had observed among some twentieth-century Friends and attenders and the plight of isolated children who had no contemporaries with whom to develop a spiritual community in which to grow up.

These were the people she hoped the tapestry would reach, but first she must develop a framework in which this could happen.

She was a trained teacher, with experience ranging from teaching home economics to children in some of the worst Manchester slums immediately after the war to using embroidery as a medium for developing a sense of colour, design, line and texture in students across a range of textile courses in a big London polytechnic. She had also run small but successful toy-making businesses for some years, so she knew how to start putting together both a practical teaching plan and initial costings for her scheme.

Her biggest problem was how to present the idea to British Quakers and secure the necessary practical and financial help.

Taunton was a small, rather quiet meeting and Anne could not imagine them backing a project of this magnitude so that she could take it to her area monthly meeting and then to Friends nationwide.

So she made a direct approach to Quaker Home Service (QHS), the central department concerned with the spiritual health of the society and with children's work. She knew people in the department, as she was her area meeting's representative at their twice-yearly consultative meeting, QHS Representative Council, and she reasoned that they might well see the value of the scheme she proposed.

When she arrived at the next representatives' meeting, in March 1981, she could contain her excitement no longer and poured out her ideas at supper to Friends from Newcastle upon Tyne, who were fascinated. One turned out to be a keen embroiderer and both could at once see the potential of the scheme. With their encouragement she asked for a slot to share her idea with the whole meeting. It was warmly received and she was encouraged to present some detailed proposals.

The seed that was to grow into the Quaker Tapestry Scheme was sown.

By early May, Anne had presented a written summary of her ideas to Elizabeth Brimelow, secretary to QHS's Children & Young People's Committee, together with embroidery samples and alternative costings for materials of different qualities. Soon afterwards she was asked to meet two Friends who were to assess her scheme on behalf of the committee.

The two Friends appointed were Irene Grey, who was one of the two Friends from Newcastle who first heard about the tapestry, and Robin Greaves, who, Anne was delighted to discover, was the daughter of Elfrida Vipont whose book Jonathan was studying. Both were convinced that Anne's project was worthwhile and have supported the tapestry ever since.

At the beginning of July, Robin wrote: 'I expect you have already heard that the Children & Young People's Committee reacted warmly to the idea of the Quaker Tapestry and decided that £1,000 should be given to you to get it going . . . I did enjoy my evening with you . . . I feel very pleased to have been in at the early stages of such an exciting venture.'

Anne had met Robin and Irene at Glenthorne, a Quaker guest house in the Lake District, where other guests had become interested, further boosting her confidence in the project. In a letter to Elizabeth Brimelow, telling of this, Anne wrote: 'By considering our history we will be drawing strength and inspiration from the past, and by creating something worthwhile we affirm our faith in the future. The best art has always honoured something greater than the individual. So our work will be in the right tradition.'

It was agreed that good quality materials should be used for the tapestry and the money was made available from a trust fund. This enabled Anne to approach weavers Talbott Potter and John Lennon, from Kingston St Mary, to design and weave a suitable fabric for the embroidery. It was to be sufficiently resilient to bear unpicking without damage and to be of a colour and texture to facilitate using the conventions of the Bayeux Tapestry, where faces and buildings are embroidered in outline, the cloth forming

Peggy Sumption

Members of Wellington and Spiceland group, the first to choose a subject and start research for a tapestry panel.

convincing stonework and skin textures.

Anne and Jonathan were putting together designs for the first panel and practising building up the pictures from the five stitches Anne had selected for the scheme. By the time the cloth came through they were ready to start.

From now on they would be both embroidering and working on research and designs for the next panels, while Anne continued to liaise with Children & Young People's Committee over launching the project nationally.

In August, Anne formally presented her scheme to Taunton meeting. A few people were interested, but not the meeting as a whole (a pattern that was often to be repeated across the country as the scheme got under way). One member of the meeting, Henry Rowntree, became treasurer when Anne received her first funds. Then, in early October, he produced the first piece of independent research, on the topography of Pendle Hill and the Pennines, to check part of Anne's design for the panel depicting Lichfield and Pendle Hill.

Peggy Sumption, a member of Taunton meeting who had been a good friend of Anne's for some years, helped by assembling and packaging embroidery kits and notelets for sale. She then ran what was to become the Tapestry Market, mainly as a mail order concern, until the end of 1985. Betty Harris, who was later a member of the Quaker Tapestry Scheme Publications Committee and did tremendous work in assembling tapestry archives,

gave general support and wrote about the scheme for the Quaker weekly magazine, *The Friend.*

Anne was also helped by two young couples who joined the meeting as attenders and whose children, together with Jonathan's younger brother and sister, Tim and Liz, swelled the children's classes. Their particularly useful contributions were in helping her to put together a slide/tape show to launch the tapestry and in testing the embroidery kits she was assembling to teach the techniques and generate funds.

The growing children's classes really enjoyed their research work as they gathered in Anne's garden to act out scenes from Quaker history, pelting one another with her husband David's socks as they sampled being in the stocks for the *Derby gaol* panel, or listening to Anne telling stories from Quaker history after which they produced delightful drawings, many of which were later used in the bottom sections of panels.

But there was a serious, adult side to this work too. Anne was determined that the panels should be accurate. Early records include a letter from the librarian of Lichfield Cathedral relating to her research for the *Lichfield and Pendle Hill* panel and a record of visiting the then librarian at Friends House, Edward Milligan.

A progress report on the tapestry given to West Somerset monthly meeting in November as part of Anne's report from QHS Representative Council resulted in two neighbouring meetings, Minehead and Wellington, putting forward ideas for panels

Betty Harris

Margaret Gardner

and in Wellington and Spiceland meetings starting research on what was to become the *Relief work overseas* panel, F7.

By March 1982, Anne was able to make a well-received presentation with slides to QHS Representative Council, as a preliminary to the national launch of the tapestry that QHS was arranging for her at residential yearly meeting at Warwick University in July.

By the time of yearly meeting, she and Jonathan had completed the first panel, *George Fox's convincement*, A1, which was mounted for display, and a second panel, *Firbank Fell: George Fox preaching*, B1, was being embroidered. Designs had been completed for three more panels, which were displayed.

Betty Harris and Anne describe the scene in an article for *The Friend*: 'Anne Wynn-Wilson went to yearly meeting weighed down with materials for exhibition. The slide/tape, which was to be such a focus of attention, was finished only the week before. She arranged an exhibition which attracted an estimated thousand viewers, passing through from morning until ten at night. The slide/tape, lasting just over a quarter of an hour . . . made a splendid introduction, concise and to the point, but wide in concept.

'Moving on, table by table, showed weaving, the selection of subjects for panels, the research work of Spiceland and Wellington meetings, embroidery instruction sheets, cartoons being drawn, samples of canvas work, crewel work and woven tapestry,

and, finally, a lively touch, two frames at which Friends could try the five stitches used and assess their own skills and abilities.

'Information and design sheets, embroidery frames, wools and notelets were on sale and the hand-woven fabric to be used for the panels on view.'

A Friend from Derby, Margaret Gardner, remembers looking into the room while Anne was setting up her exhibition and finding her at her wits' end because the slide/tape she had prepared was not working.

Margaret's husband was able to mend it and Margaret herself stayed to help Anne through the week.

'She told me about the tapestry and I was so fired with her enthusiasm, even at that very early stage, that I knew that here was, in all senses of the word, a true concern and that she was going to carry it through,' Margaret remembers.

'I asked if anyone was coming to help her and she said 'no'. So I said I would stay. There was a session that afternoon that I really wanted to go to, but I just couldn't. It was far more important to be there.

'Up on the wall was the cartoon of the *George Fox in Derby gaol* panel. At that time I was clerk of Derby meeting and I said we would embroider it. Then I went back to Derby meeting and announced this was what we had let Derby in for.'

Anne remembers her first meeting with another Margaret at Warwick, Margaret Simpson, who was

Margaret Simpson

to be secretary to the Quaker Tapestry Scheme for the next fifteen years, editor of the *Quaker Tapestry newsletter* and a prime mover in keeping the scheme running smoothly.

'Margaret is such an impressive lady that you do notice her when she comes into a room. I noticed this lady come in and look around, but she didn't speak to us. Then she came in again, and for a third time. This time, I don't know whether we spoke to her or she to us, but I know that very early on she asked what I needed, and I said 'a secretary'. She said 'I'm a secretary', and from then onwards we behaved as though it was a fait accompli.

'The first thing she did was to arrange a meeting for people interested in the scheme. The room was full to overflowing and at that meeting we established a supporters' group and found our first committee.'

Anne went home from Warwick with requests for exhibitions at yearly meetings in Ireland and Australia, offers of work for panels on various subjects and more general support from Friends across the country. She was preparing to let a panel out of her sight for the first time and was soon to be deluged with work as the scheme gathered momentum. She was also about to find herself gradually attracting a band of skilled and dedicated helpers who would enable her see the project through.

The scheme takes shape

At last, after eighteen months' careful preparation, the Quaker Tapestry Scheme had caught the imagination of Friends across the country.

If Anne had been astonished by her reception at Warwick, she was to be almost overwhelmed by Friends' immediate response to the scheme. Some 53 of the 60 or so people at the Warwick meeting in July 1982 signed up for the supporters' group and a committee was formed that met at Margaret Simpson's house in Bristol just a month later.

At this meeting, Friends formally agreed the Quaker Tapestry Committee's terms of reference and started planning their work.

Anne describes the genesis of that first committee at Warwick: 'People ask questions and it becomes obvious which people have a natural inclination to carry things forward . . . it was a kind of natural selection, rather than being nominated or selected in any way. It all worked out quite correctly. It was the right way to do it.'

Jean Brown, Ann Castle, and Maggie Goodrich, who joined Anne, Margaret and treasurer Henry Rowntree on that first committee, were all prominent Friends with considerable gifts to offer.

Jean, a keen embroiderer and wife of the then director at Woodbrooke, the Quaker college in south Birmingham, was bursting with ideas for the embroideries and instrumental in forming the tapestry groups in that area, which between them were to embroider four panels.

In the three years she served on the committee

Ann Castle working on the Simplicity *panel, D2, at Jordans meeting house.*

she provided opportunities for workshops at Woodbrooke and helped to organise exhibitions as well as encouraging Canadian Friends' interest in working on a panel when she visited their yearly meeting and other meetings in Canada in 1984.

Maggie Goodrich, then 73, who served a similar term, had just resigned from membership of the Children & Young People's Committee that had given Anne her original funding.

She describes herself as a needlewoman, rather than an embroiderer, but nonetheless took on the *Friends Provident Institution*, E11, for the Epsom group as well as serving the committee as a tireless and successful fund-raiser and ambassador for the tapestry.

Maggie was able to secure an opportunity for Anne to speak at Meeting for Sufferings, the regular representative business meeting of Quakers in Britain, which meets about nine times a year between yearly meetings. 'She was a very good speaker,' recalls Maggie. 'It changed the attitude of many Friends.'

Ann Castle, a retired occupational therapist much involved in crafts, had originally offered to produce posters for the scheme. But it was not long before she found herself completely immersed in the tapestry.

She became a teacher, embroiderer, group organiser, speaker, and poster designer. She was a tremendous support to Anne, to the committee and to embroidery groups across the country in many, many ways and, as one of the 'three Ann(e)s'

Maggie Goodrich

(she and Anne Wynn-Wilson were later joined by Ann Nichols), was one of the core group, together with Margaret Simpson, that saw the Quaker Tapestry through to completion.

As a birthright member of a dynastic Quaker family, she brought tremendously valuable knowledge of Friends and their history to the committee. 'The whole thing fascinated me,' she remembers. 'It was an all-absorbing occupation. It was my life for years.'

Ann, who involved hundreds, if not thousands, of people in the tapestry, including members of her own family, has never lost her enthusiasm for the project and was still demonstrating at exhibitions in 1997, at the age of 85.

But back to those early days. In January 1983, just five months after the Warwick exhibition, Anne Wynn-Wilson and Margaret Simpson produced the first issue of their delightful *Quaker Tapestry Newsletter* for the supporters' group, in which they were able to report that the group had grown to more than 80 and that more than 400 information leaflets had been requested.

'No week passes without my being in contact with Friends who are working on some part of the Tapestry Scheme,' wrote Anne. 'I have had letters not only from England, Scotland and Wales, but also from Australia, New Zealand, America, France, Norway, Ireland, Jersey, Saudi Arabia and Pakistan. At least 140 embroiderers have sewing kits and still more are being bought.'

Four panels were being embroidered and another four were at the design stage. Two embroidery workshops had been held and another five were being planned.

The article in *The Friend* of 15 October 1982 had asked Friends to send in suggestions for subjects for panels. By the closing date of 31 March 1983 the committee had received a heartening 404 responses.

Anne's husband, David, produced a computer print-out of the suggestions for panel subjects, which were then considered by a small sub-committee comprising Anne Wynn-Wilson, Ann Castle and Margaret Simpson.

They decided that the subjects should be organised into groups corresponding to the sections in *Christian faith and practice*, a regularly revised compilation of Friends' writings from throughout their history that is regarded by Friends as a key source of spiritual and practical guidance (now superseded by a later revision, *Quaker faith and practice*).

This would provide both a framework to ensure that the subjects of the panels reflected the breadth of Quaker belief and activity and a structure for cataloguing them.

Anne had originally planned a scheme in which 50 panels would be completed in ten years, at the rate of five a year, which she thought would be a manageable number to research, design and see through, but it was now decided that the number of panels should be increased to 60 and that this would be a maximum number.

'The first 50 per cent or so of subjects were comparatively easy to select,' recalls Anne. 'They repeated themselves several times in the list and there were obvious 'musts', such as Elizabeth Fry and William Penn.

'The next 25 per cent took more thinking about and the last few were exceedingly difficult.'

By the time the second *Newsletter* was published, in May 1983, with the centre spread devoted to panel subject selections, 42 had been chosen, 34 of which had already been adopted by groups.

Anne wrote: 'My pile of correspondence is considerable. Unfortunately it has not been possible to answer all your letters. Please accept this *Newsletter* in grateful acknowledgement if you have written to me and not received a reply.'

Four months later, at the fourth full committee meeting, little more than a year after the watershed meeting at Warwick, it was reported that four panels had been finished and four were being embroidered. There were six designs on the drawing board and three more panels were awaiting design after completion of research. Research was in progress on a further nine panels, so work had started on more than 40 per cent of panels in barely a year.

Six more subjects had been adopted by groups, another 12 accepted by the selection sub-committee and one panel had been allocated to New Zealand. Only 15 panel subjects remained for consideration.

By this time, nine embroidery workshops had been held and 28 embroidery groups were busy practising stitches or working on panels.

The *George Fox in Derby gaol* panel, F1, had gone to the Derby group, where it had been completed by a group led by Margaret Gardner, who had been such a great support to Anne the year before at Warwick.

'I recall the absolute terror I felt when I realised what I had let myself in for, an absolute novice taking on this,' says Margaret. 'Talk about going forward in faith. But, you see, I worked across the road from St Peter's Church, the steeplehouse George Fox had denounced. I walked across the market place in Derby. We lived where Justice Bennet first called us Quakers, so it seemed to me right and proper that the *Derby gaol* panel should be embroidered in Derby.'

Margaret had visited Anne in Taunton, where she was taught the stitches, and later, after she and another Friend had started the panel, attended the first Quaker Tapestry workshop in Wellington, Somerset, where she remembers meeting Frank and Ella Frisby, who worked the *Quaker Peace Action Caravan* panel, B8, in Minehead.

'At that time, I had four children, a three-storey farmhouse with stone floors, an orchard and a huge garden, but I disciplined myself to work on the tapestry every day when it was my turn,' Margaret says. 'I set it up in the dining room and after I had made the beds and done the breakfast dishes I went into the dining room and set my timer for an hour and worked on it for that time.'

Margaretta Playfair

She had hoped members of Derby meeting as a whole would be as enthusiastic as she was and keen to put their stitches in, but it was not so. Many Friends were slow to accept the value of the tapestry and her experience of working with a small group, in which perhaps one or two people did the bulk of the embroidery work, was to be repeated in many other groups across the country in the early years, including Cambridge, the destination of the second panel to leave Taunton.

This was *Swarthmoor Hall*, C1, which depicts the home of Judge and Margaret Fell and the activities that took place there. The hall was the centre of the kind of thriving commercial enterprise typical of a manor house of its day. From the 1650s, it also became the centre of the newly formed Quaker movement. Many years later, after Judge Fell died, George Fox was to marry his widow.

The panel was entrusted to Margaretta Playfair, of Cambridge. Hers had been the first letter Anne received in response to the first article (28 May 1982) in *The Friend* about the tapestry. After receiving details, she wrote Anne a treasured letter in June, saying that she and another Friend would like to take on a panel and adding: 'I do want to say how much I admire the skill and care with which you have planned everything'.

'We would both like simply to embroider, not to design,' she wrote. 'We would like to get on with it as soon as possible. I am pushing 70 and my friend is 80, so neither of us will be much good for embroidery by the time the ten years is up!'

As things turned out, Margaretta was to find herself alone in working the panel. The Friend who had intended to help discovered she was not convinced it was a good use of time and money, an attitude typical of many Friends at that time.

Margaretta visited Anne in Taunton, taking a completed sampler to show her. Like others who saw Anne's work, most of which is contemporary in style and far more advanced in technique than much of that on the tapestry panels, Margaretta was simultaneously awed and inspired by her, and, like Margaret Gardner, determined to take part in this amazing project.

Margaretta and Anne subsequently met at a convenient point between their homes in the coffee room used by the Friends of the Royal Academy, in London, where Anne gave Margaretta a couple of hours' tuition – much to the surprise of other visitors – and sent her back to Cambridge with the panel and an embroidery frame.

Margaretta set aside an hour every afternoon for the work on her panel, occasionally taking it to her local meeting and encouraging others to think about some embroidery. 'I'd set up a little exhibition at coffee time,' she remembers, 'but nobody much cared about it then, though they cared very much later – and this was true of other places, not just Cambridge. It was a very difficult start to this big scheme. Friends didn't at all see the outreach that would follow, though all three Cambridge meetings very much joined in at a later stage.

'I started working on the panel in February 1983 and by May I had something to show at yearly meeting, where they had a little exhibition. I think I had it finally finished by June or July, though they made some alterations to it after it went back to Anne, particularly to the lettering, as a designer made a new upper case alphabet.

'The faces were not easy. I had to take Margaret Fell out a few times, I kept making her so sour looking! But the fabric doesn't mind.'

As she had hoped, Margaretta had eventually gathered a group of Friends wanting to embroider and she moved on to a second panel, *Conscientious objection*, A7, which she researched while she was teaching stitches to the new group.

A member of the embroidery group had been intimately involved with the scene depicted on the panel. During the first world war she had been a pupil in the school from which the central figure, a student teacher, was removed from his class by a policeman on his eighteenth birthday. She very clearly remembered her shock at the event. The teacher himself, who was imprisoned as a conscientious objector for the remainder of the war, also gave Margaretta tremendous help with her research.

Margaretta helped with children's classes at her meeting and devoted some of her time there to telling the children stories about conscientious objection and alternative service. She encouraged them to make drawings to submit to the panel designers, some of which were used on the delightful bottom section of the panel.

Contacts of this kind, which brought panels alive for researchers and embroiderers, contributed a great deal to the educational value of the project and were cherished by the Friends involved.

After completing this panel with the Cambridge group, Margaretta was to find enthusiasm developing throughout the East Anglian meetings. She moved on to co-ordinate a third panel, *True health*, D9, in which she had a particular interest as she had been a nurse and her husband a family doctor. About 50 people in eight meetings took part.

This time, Margaretta had teaching help from Marjory Stevens, of Peterborough meeting, who had previously worked on a Leicester panel, and was herself mainly responsible for transporting the panel between groups.

'I remember once taking it by train to Peterborough, handing it to Marjory as I alighted and then smartly crossing the platform to leap on the departing Cambridge train,' says Margaretta.

'Another time Anne took it to yearly meeting in Aberdeen and kept it for six weeks while I was left to fend off workers wailing "where is our panel?" What fun it all was.'

But this was well into the future, as was the series of tapestry exhibitions in the area in 1992 – 'costed down to the last metre of fishing line for hanging the panels . . . the exhibitions themselves blissful, so relaxed and peaceful . . . attracting a steady stream of interested visitors. Well worth the many months of intensive work,' wrote Margaretta in the July 1992 *Newsletter*.

Forging community

At the heart of the tapestry scheme were the embroidery workshops. It was here that beginners learned the stitches and met people from other groups, here that research and design ideas could be discussed with others, here that work in progress could often be assessed and moved forward to its next stage and here that new entrants to the scheme often saw completed panels for the first time.

Two workshops Anne Wynn-Wilson had planned before launching the scheme, in meeting houses at Dorchester (Dorset) and at Wellington (Somerset), went ahead in the November after the 1982 Warwick exhibition. The first weekend workshop, at a Quaker residential centre, Charney Manor in Oxfordshire, took place the following April.

These were carefully planned and costed and their successful formats remained in place through most of the life of the scheme.

Anne's day workshops started over coffee at 10.30 am. Friends were then introduced to the stitches and worked for two hours before a shared lunch and for another two hours after lunch. 'Friends concentrated on the use of the embroidery frame and the structure and imaginative use of the five stitches,' wrote Anne in the first *Newsletter*.

She described a practical experiment: 'Use chain stitch in different ways to illustrate the following textures: a silk dress, a thatched roof, a sheep's fleece, a stone wall, the bark of a tree, a knitted pullover. Embroidery can be a creative craft, nothing akin to painting by numbers – more like playing music: the pattern and instructions are there, but it depends on the skill and interpretation of the artist to communicate.'

For some Friends it was hard enough to master the art of using an embroidery frame and work the five basic stitches. Others delighted in the

challenge and began to see how it would be possible to solve the technical problems posed by some of the designs while remaining within the stylistic convention Anne had evolved.

The five basic stitches, stem stitch, chain stitch, split stitch, Peking knot and Bayeux point were soon to be augmented by a new stitch for working the lettering, invented by Anne and later named Quaker stitch.

This was a breakthrough in narrative embroidery that simplified work on curved lettering. It is a corded stitch that gives a neat, uncluttered result and can be worked in different weights to suit circumstance. Its great advantage is that it avoids the stray ends that result from working lettering in stem stitch, as on the Bayeux Tapestry.

Quaker stitch has been accepted by the Royal College of Needlework as a new stitch and its use is spreading far beyond the Quaker Tapestry. Together with the other stitches used in the tapestry, it is described in detail in Anne's book, *Quakers in stitches*.

This slim, illustrated volume describes all the techniques necessary to complete pictures in the style of the Quaker Tapestry, from the important foundation techniques of how to transfer designs to calico backing fabric, how to mount the embroidery fabric on the calico and the whole on an embroidery frame to details of working the individual stitches, building up three layers of embroidery and creating an illusion of perspective.

To begin with, Anne led the workshops herself, but was soon joined by Ann Castle, and, later, Ann Nichols, who, after guiding the Nottingham group through embroidering *The voyage of the Woodhouse*, A5, was so delighted with the scheme that she devoted much of her retirement to the tapestry.

Ann Nichols had originally trained as a librarian, but later, as her family grew up, found her vocation

Ann Nichols setting out a three-dimensional model of panel A1,
George Fox's convincement, *in preparation for a class at a workshop at*
Lattendales on how to use the tapestry to teach children.

at the age of 35 and retrained as a teacher, ending up as a headmistress.

She loved embroidery, which had become one of her specialisations during her teacher training course and which she continued to study and teach throughout her career, but it was the use Anne Wynn-Wilson was making of it that drew her to the Quaker Tapestry.

The first workshop she and other members of the Nottingham group attended was a joint one with the Leicester group, which was working on the *Stephen Grellet* panel, B5. 'It was from this first meeting with Leicester Friends, who came from a different monthly meeting, from having workshops with them and becoming very involved with them that I realised what really interested me,' Ann explained.

'Although the embroidery was very important, and I loved it, it was the opportunity for ordinary Quakers to meet that I really enjoyed. Leicester were at about the same stage as us, just beginning the embroidery, and they occasionally would ask me for advice. It was the blind leading the blind at first, but most groups only needed confidence and reassurance they were on the right lines. I could do that side of it.'

So Ann gradually became one of the embroidery teachers, joined the committee in March 1983, and soon took responsibility for panels down the eastern side of the country and for the Canadian panel.

Ann Castle, after a steep learning curve as a

tapestry teacher when she took the *Elizabeth Fry and the patchwork quilts* panel, E6, across Australia in winter 1983-84, worked mainly with groups in the south of England. She also oversaw other groups, including that in her childhood home, Darlington, which embroidered *Bankering*, E3. Ann travelled with Anne Wynn-Wilson to New England and to Ireland.

Anne Wynn-Wilson was the main contact for groups down the western corridor of England, and for Wales, Ireland and Scotland. She also liaised with Friends working panels in other countries and worked closely with the other embroidery teachers.

The weekend workshops, at which all three Ann(e)s would often teach together as the scheme expanded, were held two or three times a year in venues across the country and Friends often travelled considerable distances to attend.

Bookings and accommodation were organised by various members of the committee at different times, although Margaret Simpson was responsible for much of this work and for welfare arrangements for participants during residential workshops.

Requirements included a secure workroom with good natural lighting for embroidery work as well as reasonable prices and suitable accommodation. Charney Manor was used most frequently, though successful workshops were held in many other places.

Friends usually met on the Friday evening for supper, followed by an introductory talk and slide

A tapestry workshop at Hammersmith, London.

show from Anne Wynn-Wilson. The next morning, the format would depend entirely on the needs of those present, with opportunities for beginners to learn the stitches, making small samplers under supervision, and for groups to set up new panels, receive advice about embroideries in progress or consult over research and design.

In the afternoon Friends would have the choice of continuing their embroidery or free time. There would be more work between tea and supper with recreations such as story-telling after supper. On Sunday morning there would be a closing session and meeting for worship.

Anne Wynn-Wilson taught mainly through the kind of day and weekend workshops described and through private tutorials at her home, such as those received by Friends from Derby and Cambridge. Ann Castle and Ann Nichols developed their own teaching styles, as did other teachers as the scheme developed.

Ann Castle tended to introduce panels at area monthly meetings and then work closely with local groups at informal meetings in people's homes or meeting houses. She would help with any problems and collect and deliver panels as they moved between groups, perhaps with a little work on them herself in between.

Ann Nichols's style is described by Anne Wynn-Wilson as one primarily concerned with forging community. 'I am full of admiration for the way she seemed to make all her groups into very supportive communities,' she says. Perhaps not surprisingly, it was Ann Nichols who often sorted out the

inevitable difficulties caused by misunderstandings or disagreements over panels and who proved a tremendous support to the last few groups who were still finishing panels when the main thrust of activity was going into exhibitions.

Her ready empathy with others is illustrated by her account of her first meeting with Anne Wynn-Wilson during a holiday in the west country. 'I phoned her and said: "I've written to you and written to you, can I come and visit you?"', she remembers. 'When I went to her house we spoke the same language almost immediately and I could see at once why my letters hadn't been answered. The poor woman was absolutely snowed under. She had piles and piles of unanswered letters.'

Ann left with the *Woodhouse* panel, A5, for the Nottingham group. Anne Wynn-Wilson had been about to embroider it herself as a demonstration panel and it was already mounted on its frame and ready to start – though with a key quotation missing. 'Very often insights for quotations came while we were working on panels,' explains Ann Nichols.

She took to the scheme at once. 'The groups I enjoyed working with most were the ones where we made it a social occasion. We learned a terrific amount from the talk that went on about the panels and about the insights,' she says. 'We also learned about each other because when you are relaxed and when you've got your eyes down, embroidering, you can let what's on your mind come out. I think that helped a lot of people.'

Ann's groups were particularly good at finding

Part of The voyage of the Woodhouse *panel, A5.*

opportunities for people. The story of the purple fish recounted on page 7, itself an example of Ann's flexibility, could never have happened had she not found a way of making a children's section on the *Woodhouse* panel in the first place.

'We received the panel ready designed,' she explained. 'If it had been our design there would have been a strip for the children, but as there wasn't I asked them what they would like to do and they said the fish – so that became their section.'

A Friend in the same group, who had been disabled in a motor accident, asked to embroider the waves and spray. When she had finished and the embroiderers were admiring her work, Ann remembers her saying: 'I enjoyed it because it took me back to my dancing.'

Each embroidery group had a group leader, who was responsible for overseeing the panel on a day-to-day basis as well as organising oversight as necessary from one of the teachers. Some groups rarely asked for help from the Ann(e)s as they had particularly skilled leaders, others needed more frequent oversight.

York group, which embroidered *John Woolman*, A6, received help from all three Ann(e)s and from Faith Rodger at various times, mainly due to a combination of their quest for perfection and their pleasure in working as a group, which led to comparatively slow progress.

'In the end, we had to set a limit on the number of times we would unpick things,' they admitted, as they joyously, if nervously, entered into the spirit

of the project, organising workshops and an exhibition as well as embroidering.

Leeds group, in contrast, was one of those which was perhaps a little isolated from the rest of the scheme, simply because it was so self-sufficient. Rapid progress was made with the embroidery of *Merchants*, D6, mainly by Pat Butterfield, Bette Dewhurst and three other Friends, who did not ask for much teaching support. Their policy of taking the panel to every local meeting and encouraging people to add stitches resulted in contributions from about 70 per cent of members of their monthly meeting, a remarkable achievement probably not matched by any other group.

Another approach was that of the Bakewell and Sheffield group (*Coalbrookdale*, D4), comparative latecomers to the scheme, who threw themselves in with enthusiasm with several members taking part in holidays and stewarding exhibitions as well as embroidering their panel.

Ray Noyce, of Bakewell meeting, one of whose ancestors had worked in Coalbrookdale, a centre of the iron industry in the eighteenth century, joined the Quaker Tapestry Scheme committee as treasurer and later became responsible for storage and transport of finished panels. Faith Rodger, of Sheffield meeting, became an embroidery teacher for the scheme in her area while both she and her sister, Margaret Lawson, became members of the Quaker Tapestry at Kendal Publications Committee.

The tapestry holidays, which were a great success and hugely enjoyed by their participants, started in

October 1985 at Glenthorne. The format, a combination of work on the tapestry, organised outings or free time, talks, walks and convivial meals was carefully, though unobtrusively, planned to provide a relaxed atmosphere.

From the start, Friends from outside the tapestry scheme were brought in to introduce the participants to new skills. Anita Billington, who had been a great support to Anne when she was getting the tapestry scheme off the ground, brought yoga to the first holiday.

'The yoga was an event before breakfast that some of us were surprised to find we enjoyed,' wrote Alison Burnley, one of the Scottish Friends who oversaw that country's panels (*Oaths*, A9, and *Publishers of Truth*, B4) and a member of the Quaker Tapestry Scheme committee from 1986 to 1990. 'Anita Billington encouraged us to do only what we were able and, in good Quaker tradition, not to be in competition with anyone else.'

At another tapestry holiday, in 1987 at Charbonnières, in the Pêrche region of France, the theme was storytelling through the crafts.

This was a wonderful enterprise, which built on the success of the Glenthorne holiday and successfully combined embroidery with a wide variety of excursions and activities so that embroiderers' friends and partners could also enjoy a week in the lovely old château in its 80-acre park.

Peter and Margaret Whittle were invited to be host and hostess. 'They contributed much to the success of the week not only by acting as hosts and smoothing our way in practical matters, but also by waking us up most delightfully each morning with their part singing,' recalls Ann Cuming, a novice embroiderer who much enjoyed her holiday, reported enthusiastically to *The Friend*, and became a staunch supporter of the tapestry.

Elements of the programme ranged from workshops in basic embroidery and lettering to advanced creative embroidery and design. They also included storytelling, sketching and outings to look at architecture. For many, the highlight of the week was a visit to the Bayeux Tapestry, where preliminary arrangements were made for the Quaker Tapestry to be exhibited in the same building in 1990.

There was also, of course, work in progress on the Quaker Tapestry panels, which included laying the foundations of the embroidery on *The world family of Friends* panel, and the pleasure of good food and good company in pleasant surroundings.

There was just one more of these adventurous tapestry holidays, in 1988 at The Mount School, in York, after which the committee was immersed in preparing for major exhibitions as the embroidery scheme moved towards completion.

Research proves a challenge

Work on the panels, together with experience at workshops and with research groups was providing Anne Wynn-Wilson and the committee with tremendous feedback about the needs and abilities of the Friends who were becoming involved.

While many groups were adhering to the embroidery guidelines and asking for help if they got stuck, a few embroiderers produced work that, although beautiful in itself, was outside the stylistic conventions of the tapestry scheme. One or two others found it difficult to reach the required technical standards.

Some researchers produced clear, well focused ideas. At the other end of the spectrum Anne received from one group a few scribbled ideas on a paper bag.

At the same time, mounting enthusiasm for the project led to mounting piles of letters at Anne's home, which she was finding more and more difficult to deal with as she divided her time between the myriad demands of the tapestry, her family, moving house and her toymaking business.

Something had to give, and she closed her toy business in return for a small honorarium from tapestry funds. The extra time released was soon devoured by the tapestry. By May 1984, all 60 subjects had been allocated, only seven panels remained for adoption, seven had been completed and research and design work was gathering momentum.

Perhaps not surprisingly, the enthusiasm of the earlier *Newsletters* was now tempered with reports of practical difficulties: 'As more groups complete their research, in Taunton we suffer from a mounting pile of design work.

'We have tried co-operating with other designers, but differing design styles have complicated rather than eased the situation, although we are still looking for compatible design help.'

While the obvious bottleneck was design, this was compounded by the underlying difficulties associated with many groups' research.

In devising the scheme, most of Anne's energy had gone into the embroidery and the feasibility of the enterprise as a whole. She believed that in the instruction sheets sent out to groups she had made clear the research requirements, but she had reckoned without the particular and very human enthusiasms of many of those who adopted panels.

Hours of work by individuals and groups on the pride and joy of their locality, such as Wellington's work on Spiceland, the Quaker training centre for war relief workers during the second world war, Leicester's local railway interests, Leeds' work on local merchants and Newcastle upon Tyne's view of Friends' industrial base was significantly widened to gain a broader perspective of the topics.

Some groups' favourite quotations or subject ideas had to be relinquished as they had been used by other groups. In one case, an agreed and carefully researched subject was subsequently dropped by the committee in favour of another in the interests of balance of subject matter.

The work was never wasted, for the Friends concerned and their meetings made good use of it, but there is no denying either the disappointment of those involved or their determination to make the best of their new situation.

Sidmouth group, for example, whose research on Edward Burrough was never used, was offered the *John Bright* panel, B3, ready for stitching. Group leader Rowan Easterbrook was initially horrified. 'I was a bit anti-political at the time,' she recalls. 'I didn't want anything to do with it. But we had agreed to do a panel so we got going and once I started reading about John Bright I was inspired.' Fortunately her closest co-worker was not impeded

Marjorie Fishenden with a ceramic wall hanging made by Leicester children using some of the embroidery group's information about local railways.

by the same emotions and was a great encouragement.

Leicester Friends, who had to relinquish their local interests in favour of a national scene on *Railways*, D7, made a pamphlet out of their local railway information and their children made a big, beautiful ceramic wall hanging. The group also embroidered a copy of their panel for the meeting house, in which a treasured drawing that had been left out of the panel for the Quaker Tapestry was reinstated. Darlington, who had expected to do railways, but were too late in formally adopting the panel, soon became fascinated by *Bankering*, E3, a national subject with a good local story that they thoroughly enjoyed researching.

Groups with clearly defined subjects often fared best. It was sometimes easier to identify the most important aspects of an individual's contribution to Quaker work or the wider good than to select the most appropriate aspects of broader subjects.

But even here there were surprises. Researchers in Leicester discovered that the famous and much-loved story of Stephen Grellet preaching in a deserted American lumber camp and unknowingly converting a man who overheard him, which is suggested by the centrepiece of their first panel, B5, was probably not true. Group leader Rosa Aylward determined that the illustration would have to go, though the committee subsequently decided it should stay as the sentiment reflected Grellet's character so clearly.

What was left out is often as interesting as what went in. Researchers working on the panel concerned with Friends' part in the campaign for the abolition of the slave trade (*The slave trade*, F3) had to face the fact that before British Quakers began to take action in 1783 there had been a decade when, despite pressures from Friends in America, they had appeared over-cautious – though when they finally did start campaigning, their contribution was, as shown in the panel, both vigorous and successful.

Until the nineteenth century, many Friends were brewers. The natural place for this was on the panel *Innocent trades*, D5, the title of which came from an eighteenth-century description of useful industries without military connections.

Newcastle Friends, who embroidered that panel but did not choose its title, argued that many twentieth-century people looking at it would not realise that beer was the staple drink before safe drinking water and that Quaker brewers were models of probity in an often corrupt industry. They would be further confused if they were aware of the strong Quaker presence in the campaign against the evils of drink, which began in the mid-nineteenth century.

In the early stages of the scheme Anne Wynn-Wilson supplied forms on which to submit drawings but by 1984 she was finding this led to complications. Her plea in the *Newsletter* was for clarity in thinking: 'I would ask research groups to send only data supporting a considered approach to their subject, to describe the point they wish to illustrate, and to provide photographs and details, but no finished drawings.

'The panels must not show misplaced pride and nostalgia. It may be helpful to consider the content of each panel as honouring past Friends by recognising their experience as a beacon to guide our attempt to cope with the problems of today, bearing in mind that people and ideas are probably more important than buildings.'

Buildings soon became more important than expected. Friends wanted to see their own meeting houses on the meeting houses panels, C4-C6, and the postcard illustrating *Schools*, C7, is one of the best-sellers in exhibition shops. These four panels became peripatetic, in the care of the embroidery teachers, rather than being adopted by particular groups. As far as possible, Friends embroidered their own meeting houses and the schools that they had attended.

The *Coalbrookdale*, D4, *Woodbrooke*, B6, and *The Netherlands 1940-5*, F22, panels also used buildings to good effect, though the design of the *Netherlands* panel, which shows two houses in which Jewish people were sheltered by Friends during the second world war, was something of a compromise for the embroiderers.

Several submissions had been made by Friends from the Netherlands, ranging from pre-war international education to present-day involvement in the international friendship organisation Mothers for Peace. They included different aspects of wartime activity under occupation and the crisis of conscience faced by a people committed to truth and to the concept of 'that of God in everyone' during this period.

The final design, made by Anne Wynn-Wilson from Dutch Friends' photographs and drawings, focuses on one aspect of the wartime activity, hiding Jewish people in Quaker homes. The buildings represent activities too complicated to depict in the embroidery, while the canalside building and the flags give the panel a particularly Dutch flavour.

Miep Lieffinck, who embroidered this building,

Harold Nichols

tells how another Friend was concerned that it looked crooked and wondered if it should be taken out and embroidered again. They couldn't decide and showed Friends in The Hague meeting, one of whom resolved the issue in a very practical way by saying: 'Go and look at the houses. They are all 400 years old. They are all crooked. It's just as it should be!'

Many groups were able to follow Anne's guidelines and produced excellent research and clear ideas for design. But for those who couldn't, there were often long delays while research was checked and augmented and hours were spent visualising and producing acceptable designs.

From 1984 onwards, help came from Ann Nichols's husband, Harold, who became an invaluable member of the Quaker Tapestry Scheme committee. He was a skilled researcher, interested in Friends' history, who spent a great deal of time checking and augmenting research from groups, either by advising them in their work or, when necessary, completing research himself.

Significant contributions were also made by several others. David Butler, who still helps with the tapestry exhibition at Kendal, worked on research and design for three panels, *Meeting houses overseas*, C5, *Meeting houses in the community*, C6, *and Schools*, C7. His illustrated booklet, *Quaker meeting houses,* is one of a series on different subjects published by the Quaker Tapestry Scheme.

Writer and Quaker historian Elfrida Vipont was a useful consultant, as was Ormerod Greenwood, a well-known Friend who was a powerful supporter of the tapestry from the start and author of the first book about it, *The Quaker Tapestry*, published in 1990. Anne Wynn-Wilson contributed to research throughout and, at a later stage, Edward Milligan, former librarian at Friends House, became closely involved.

Members of the tapestry committee and participants at workshops often contributed ideas that helped move research and design forward, as did many other people, often by chance.

Sometimes existing research led to a panel. Mary

*A model of Milford Haven meeting house made for an
exhibition of Quaker Tapestry panels in the town.*

Mason, of Plymouth, was researching a book based
on family records about three Friends who visited
the Czar in 1854 in an attempt to prevent the
Crimean war. She suggested the story would make
a panel, *Delegation to the Czar 1854*, F5, which was
designed by her and her daughter, Deborah, and
subsequently used to illustrate the cover of her
book, *Sleigh ride to Russia*.

Researcher Stephen Griffith suggested the
Milford Haven panel, F12, which was later used on
the cover of his book about the unusual history of
this Pembrokeshire town, which was founded by
Quaker whalers from Nantucket and is built on an
American grid plan.

The substantial section on Quakers in the town's
fascinating museum contains a model of the
Friends meeting house, which was built by a
member of the meeting for the exhibition of the
Quaker Tapestry held in the town in 1992, at which
34 panels were displayed.

Maggie Goodrich, whose husband worked for the
insurance company Friends Provident, used a
recently published history of the company as the
basis for her research for panel E11 and was given
both practical and financial help by the company.

Even where research was comparatively simple it
could give rise to unexpected problems and
appropriate solutions. *Vigils for peace*, F17, was
designed from a photograph of a real vigil – but the
group that had originally planned to embroider it,
which received it during a miners' strike, thought it

too confrontational, too like a picket line, and it
was embroidered by another group, Uxbridge.

The leader of the group that took it on saw things
quite differently. 'I am active in the peace
movement, have taken part in many vigils (though
not this one), and badly wanted our meeting to do
a panel on this subject,' she said. 'Secondly, I am a
painter, who had already moved from paint to
fabric stitching, and the use of Appleton wools, so
rich in colour and pleasant to work with, gave
another dimension to my work. I have since done
other pictures in the medium connected with peace
work.'

Anne Wynn-Wilson speaks of the profound
effect researching *George Fox: Lichfield, Pendle Hill*,
D1, had on her own spiritual life, describing it as 'a
very personal panel', while she refers to 'an
amazing experience teaching the children' as she
worked on the basis of a peaceable life for *George
Fox in Derby gaol*, F1. 'I was shifting my ideas at the
same time as they were shifting theirs,' she says.
'The depth of their insight is perhaps most clearly
illustrated by their later drawings of the man in
prison for *Persecution in Oxford*, D3.'

Many groups submitted their own designs, some
of which, such as Daphne Boothby's for *John
Bellers*, E2, came from professional artists, who
liaised with Anne throughout to ensure their
designs would be appropriate. Wendy Gillett, who
designed the *Milford Haven* panel, F12, went on to
design panel A6, *John Woolman* (with drawings

from York children) and to draw panels E1, *George Fox at Ulverston: healing*, designed by Anne Wynn-Wilson, and A8, *Manchester Conference 1895*.

'Teamwork of this kind was an excellent way of combining different people's skills,' observes Anne.

Some submitted designs were rejected completely. Some, such as Leeds' *Merchants*, D6, were substantially accepted and elements of others could sometimes be included in final designs.

'Of course design was the bottleneck,' says Anne Wynn-Wilson. 'Some people seemed to feel you could make a design just by sitting down for the evening and doing it. I reckon that a design, even if everything went well, took at least a full week's work. Then it had to be accepted by the committee and the group.

'Joe McCrum, a marvellous retired designer and ex-head of design at Glasgow College of Art, who worked on nineteen of the panels for us, reckoned every design he did would have cost at least £250 worth of his time if he had charged for it – and that was in the early 1980s.

'I don't think people realised that it wasn't only the design, it was finding the concept. For the *Stephen Grellet* panel, for example, the research was done extremely well, but there was so much and it was such a marvellous life, it was difficult to see how to condense it into one panel – it needed an illustrated book.'

Some influential Friends appear on more than one panel. George Fox features on five, Elizabeth Fry's work was split between two panels (E5 and E6) and William Penn appears on two – *The Penn and Meade trial 1670*, F2, and *Penn and Pennsylvania*, F11.

Every design was the result of weeks, months and sometimes years of patient gathering of information, piecing together stories, teasing out quotations and seeking the catalyst that would clarify thinking and enable the designer to get to work.

Designers at work

Anne Wynn-Wilson with The prism, *the title panel of the Quaker Tapestry.*

Anne Wynn-Wilson describes her own approach to design as thorough research followed by a willingness to break away from reality to tell the story. In *George Fox's convincement*, A1, for example, she describes him as sitting in the middle thinking, surrounded by influences on that thinking. 'There is a logic in the design that you couldn't photograph,' she points out. 'It broke away from physical reality to tap a greater reality.'

The title panel, *The prism*, which includes every colour used in the tapestry scheme, and the final panel, *The world family of Friends*, were both designed on the principle of breaking away from reality, but were special cases.

'It took me three years to see how to express a suitable idea for the title panel,' says Anne. 'I sketched odd ideas over the years, but the tapestry made such tremendous demands on my time it was never possible to just go away and be creative. It was only when I had a whole week free while my daughter was on holiday and I was baby-sitting her

Siamese kittens that I was really free to clear my mind.

'I started by meditation and listening to music and was able to reach a different level of perception, which is why that particular design speaks on so many different levels, the centring and expanding of experience, a symbol of completeness with infinity at either end.

'The spiral is the link between the first panel and the last panel. In the title panel the spiral represents the spiritual experience of the Religious Society of Friends and in the last panel the spiral represents the energy of Friends' world organisations.

'I started the design for the last panel by drawing spirals with charcoal on newspaper. The idea of the oak tree came from the Family Gathering of Friends at Waterford, Ireland in 1986, which was attended by Friends from around the world. During the last evening's entertainment a most wonderful tree construction was brought on stage and the children portrayed the life that goes on in the tree: the insects, the birds and the animals.

'The idea for the children's drawings of 'me and my friends' came from a conversation with a Friend. Children from as many countries as I was able to make contacts in sent drawings. As I learned to expect, all the children drew humanity in the same way, wherever they came from – just as I had previously discovered that children all over the world use the convention of showing, for example, a horse that has passed by drawing it without a head.

'The embroidery was equally cosmopolitan. *The world family of Friends* panel was embroidered in Switzerland, Scotland, America and England, but people from all over the world put stitches in.'

It was not until after the first panels had been designed that Anne recognised the contribution that could be made by children's drawings, which were first used in *Elizabeth Fry and the patchwork quilts*, E6, and *Richard Seller*, A4. At this time she was working on research with children in Taunton meeting.

For the *Richard Seller* panel, their source of information was *A book of Quaker saints*, by Violet Hodgkin. 'There must have been five weeks' worth of marvellous stories there that really caught the children's imagination,' she remembers. 'We were working on it near Armistice Day and getting the feel of the dilemma that the poor man was in fitted remarkably well with thinking about more modern conscientious objectors.

'I was working with very young children and I was surprised by their understanding of a very complex story and how much could be illustrated by using their drawings in the bottom section of the panel. Most awful things happened to the poor man. At one stage he was taken up into the rigging and dropped to the deck. If I tried to illustrate this it would prove very difficult, but the child's drawing is very simple and conveys totally the broken nature of a body that's dropped from a height.'

The panel, which was embroidered by Taunton children and Bull Street meeting in Birmingham, was designed by Joe McCrum, whose offer of help resulted from one of those extraordinary coincidences that blessed the Quaker Tapestry Scheme.

Joe, who lived in a village outside Taunton, had met some Quakers from the town who had attended an ecumenical service in the village

Joe McCrum, who worked on the design of 19 panels, with some abstracts he painted in his eighties.

church, found them very friendly and decided to visit Taunton meeting to see what a Quaker meeting for worship was like. On that very Sunday, Anne asked Friends if they knew anyone who might help design panels for the tapestry and Joe offered.

'My second wife had recently died, just a year after we had moved to Somerset from Glasgow,' he explains. 'It was something to do and it was most interesting.'

One of his first tasks was to design a new alphabet for the tapestry. He was not impressed with the upper case lettering Anne was using, though he liked the lower case. She was delighted to accept the new alphabet.

They soon established a method of working in which Anne would invite Joe to lunch and afterwards tell him the story that was to be depicted on the panel. Joe would make rough sketches and then go away and make his design, using any source materials Anne could offer, supplemented by his own research into costumes and other contemporary sources. This suited both of them as Anne loves storytelling and Joe loves stories.

He particularly enjoyed the story of the mischievous Gurney sisters holding up a mail coach, depicted in the bottom section of *Elizabeth Fry*, E5. The ships for *The voyage of the Woodhouse*, A5, and the coach for *Bankering*, E3, also brought much pleasure.

Industrial design was a strong thread in Joe's own career. As a young man he worked on locomotive designs for British Rail. His other industrial design work ranged from cookers to light fittings (which he also made). He worked for some years for the Council of Industrial Design,

Daphne Boothby (left) modelling for her design for the figure of John Bellers (right), panel E2.

now the Design Council, and is an accomplished artist, with work ranging from particularly strong watercolour landscapes to a linked series of abstracts painted in his eighties.

Joe worked on 19 panels, some entirely designed by himself and others in collaboration with Anne. They worked well together and produced designs exhibiting remarkable strength and clarity with an inspired approach to the use of symbols to place the action – a capstan and coils of rope on *Elizabeth Fry and the patchwork quilts*, E6, and a hint of rigging on *Richard Seller*, A4, to indicate events on board ships, the hand of God on *The voyage of the Woodhouse*, A5, and the delicate stonework and bars that suggest prison in *Conscientious objection*, A7, and *James Parnell: Meeting for Sufferings*, A3.

The bold designs of *Coalbrookdale*, D4, enhanced by the Bakewell and Sheffield groups' meticulous work on the smoke and flames, and *Simplicity*, D2, with the striking central figure embroidered by Ann Castle, are firm favourites with Friends, as is *Marriage*, C8, framed prints of which are often given as wedding presents.

Soon after Joe stepped down from the design team, yet another stroke of good fortune brought Margery Levy to Anne's attention. Margery had specialised in embroidery and enamelling at art college before going on to teach and to work as a silversmith and enameller. She was a birthright Friend who had wanted to take part in the tapestry since it started but had been prevented by the need to care for her mother-in-law.

'I think I expected to embroider,' says Margery,

who soon after her mother-in-law's death went to a tapestry weekend at Charney Manor. 'But the nearest group I knew about was in Southampton and it soon became clear that I would be more useful as a designer.'

She has a clear memory of her visit to Charney, which coincided with a visit by Friends from the Dublin and Waterford groups, who were working on the design of their panel, *Ireland: the great hunger 1845-8*, E8. Another panel at the design stage at that workshop was *James Nayler*, A2, which Margery was asked to draw from a design by Anne Wynn-Wilson and Margaret Simpson.

'I can't remember quite how much of *James Nayler* I did,' recalls Margery, 'I worked on it again much later on so it was probably quite a lot. The bit that sticks in my mind was co-opting one of the men from the Irish group, Jim Sexton, and persuading him to be tied up and lie on the floor to serve as a model for the figure of James Nayler.'

Margery liked to draw from life whenever possible and later used her husband as a model for figures, such as the man digging the garden in *Industrial welfare*, D11.

A variation on this technique was that used by Daphne Boothby in the design of *John Bellers*, E2, where she had herself photographed sitting writing at a table as a model for the figure of Bellers in the top left-hand corner of the panel.

Margery, who designed seven panels and drew sections of others, found *True health*, D9, and *Industrial welfare*, D11, panels particularly tricky to design as there was so much to say. 'I wish I had

had time to do some embroidery first,' she says. 'They do seem a bit cluttered.' They certainly provided the embroiderers (Cambridge and Bournville) with a challenge, particularly in the small lettering.

The decorative ribbon lettering and central message on the *Industrial welfare* panel were typical of contemporary decoration on items such as biscuit tins and Margery particularly delights in the gold spectacles added to one of the figures by a member of the Bournville group. She, like Anne, loves to see a sense of humour in the panels and gleefully points out a catapult hanging out of a boy's pocket, added by a member of the Salisbury group to *William Allen*, E12, another of Margery's designs.

Margery, who describes herself somewhat harshly as prosaic and practical in her approach, produced a wonderfully exotic design for *Service overseas*, B7, complete with tropical trees and pagoda, exploited to the full by an equally exotic use of colour by the embroiderers as it made its way round various groups as a peripatetic panel. *Mary Fisher*, B2, is a beautifully bold design of hers, on which she did a little embroidery with the Southampton group.

Her design for *Relief work: British Isles*, F6, evokes a tremendous sense of movement, something achieved in a quite different way on *George Fox at Ulverston: healing*, E1, designed by Anne Wynn-Wilson and drawn by Wendy Gillett.

'The Ulverston panel was designed long after the other George Fox ones', says Anne. 'I wanted to draw it myself but never had time. Then, when Wendy Gillett was offering her services, I realised she could draw these figures very much better than me. I talked to her about my idea of the triangular design and she interpreted it perfectly, with the healing mind at the top of the triangle overcoming the conflict, which was of a lower order. I embroidered George Fox and shared the embroidery of the mob with a lot of people, including Wendy Gillett, who specialised in faces and reflections. It was a peripatetic panel.'

Wendy, who is not only an artist but also designed most of her own house in Wales, is responsible for one of the most painterly designs

Margery Levy

in the tapestry, *Nantucket and Milford Haven*, F12, which combines strong focal points with an extraordinarily evocative suggestion of the wet Prescelly Hills, a favourite haunt of the poet Waldo Williams, beautifully embroidered by Wendy herself.

She was a new attender at Milford Haven meeting when designs for the panel were being discussed and found that working on the tapestry drew her into the meeting, whose members were keen to do a panel. After sending off a tentative design to Anne, Wendy realised it would not be suitable and produced several more drawings of individual events that might combine into a panel.

Most members of the meeting were already practising the embroidery stitches at weekly meetings, under instruction from Margaret Redpath, who had attended a weekend course at Charney Manor. They now met two or three times to consider what should be on the panel and, with Wendy, gradually moved towards the final design. 'I had originally thought we were considering the history of Milford Haven,' remembers Wendy, 'but suddenly realised it was the spirit behind the history that mattered. It was working together on it that made it what it was.'

Margaret Crosby's *Pilgrimages*, C9, and Daphne Boothby's *John Bellers*, E2, are two panels that stand out to Anne Wynn-Wilson as ones that reflect their designers' painting skills. 'You can see Daphne paints in oils,' she says, 'Queen Anne seems almost to have been squeezed out of a tube – and Margaret Crosby's drawing of figures is outstanding.'

Anne remembers designing 15 panels herself and sharing design work with others on another 24, a substantial contribution. She also had some design input, especially lettering, on many other panels when the designs were submitted to the production committee for approval or panels were embroidered by groups in her care.

An example of the difficulty in trying to be precise in attributing design or embroidery work is *Meeting houses*, C4, where the buildings were drawn by Maurice Green of Totnes, an architect, and the figures, based on members of Taunton meeting, by Joe McCrum. Anne was responsible for placing the figures and making a montage of Maurice Green's drawings. Anne's oak tree serves to recall that some Friends met in the open air before they had meeting houses.

Much of the design help came from non-Quakers, including Maurice Green. Joe McCrum, though he attended Taunton meeting for a while and much appreciates Quaker values, returned to his village church when he remarried.

They, like several others, were inspired by the tapestry and wanted to help. This was also to be the case with embroiderers across the country, such as Beryl Dungey, the most skilled embroiderer in the Dorking & Horsham monthly meeting group that worked *Penn and Pennsylvania*, F11, and Sheila Fraser, a member of staff at the Royal School of Needlework, who worked on *Unemployment*, E10, with the Hemel Hempstead group.

Sheila came to the tapestry in a quest to learn Quaker stitch and enjoyed a tapestry holiday at Charbonnières as well as working with Hemel Hempstead. Beryl, who knew members of the Dorking & Horsham group through peace work with the Campaign for Nuclear Disarmament, not only brought embroidery skills, but also embodied the kind of tact and gentleness displayed by many of the unsung heroes and heroines who helped to hold the scheme in balance.

'I didn't unpick anything at all because I thought it would be a wrong thing to do,' she says. 'But one thing that troubled me very much was that one or two of the faces people had done were quite grotesque. I did add a few stitches to make them more human.'

The central Production Committee did its best to serve its designers equally well, whether professionals or those from the embroidery groups, but it was sometimes difficult and, at worst, impossible. In the end the tapestry embraced a tremendous variety of design approaches, sometimes stretching to the limit the ability of the cohesion of the embroidery conventions and the lettering to hold them together.

Occasionally toes were trodden upon, but the great joy of the scheme itself and the loyalty of those taking part almost always won through as peace was restored or a compromise reached and embroidery could at last begin.

Stitching begins

The joys of receiving final designs were rarely followed immediately by the pleasures of putting in the first few stitches. There was careful preparation to be done before embroidery could start.

First the design had to be transferred from a full-sized tracing of the original drawing to a piece of calico, which was then carefully stitched to the back of the woollen fabric on which the panel was to be embroidered. This had the advantage of strengthening the completed panel as well as providing a means to transfer the design.

The outline of the design was then stitched through from the calico to the wool, using a technique known as trapunto, so that the embroiderers could see their pictures from the front of the panel.

Trapunto is more usually employed in quilting than in embroidery, but proved very successful on the tapestry panels where the outlines not only needed to be clear, but often became an integral part of the design, as on upper case letters where they contained the decorative Quaker stitch.

As is so often the case with things that look easy, such seemingly simple tasks proved much more tricky than they appeared. It was soon apparent that the first stages needed always to be done under supervision from a teacher, who would show the embroiderers how to stitch the lines through using colours related to the colours to be used for each part of the final embroidery.

One group, with very experienced embroiderers as leaders, went its own way and would not attach the calico to the woollen fabric during a workshop. Later, they fixed it the wrong way, so that the warp ran horizontally and the weft vertically. The embroiderers did not take their work in progress to workshops and none of the teachers saw the panel until it was half finished.

It was beautifully embroidered but did not match the other panels as the warp so clearly ran the wrong way. It would have to be worked again. Another group, Bakewell and Sheffield, were glad to take it on, starting again from scratch and melding into a particularly happy team.

Such disasters rarely happened, but even where groups and their teachers carried out the preparation work meticulously and followed the grain of the fabric with great care while embroidering, the mounted panels sometimes appear slightly uneven – a great disappointment to the embroiderers and not always easily explained. Perhaps it may sometimes be due to variations in tension in the stitching or to difficulties in tensioning the panel evenly when mounting.

Anne Wynn-Wilson transferred the designs, but the job of preparing the fabrics, which was very time-consuming for the embroidery teachers, was eventually taken over centrally by a group of Friends from Bradford-on-Avon meeting, Anne's home meeting after she moved from Taunton. They became expert at this vital work, which enabled the teachers to give more time to teaching.

It soon became apparent that it was important to do all the outlining work early on, rather than just enough to get going so that the 'real' work could start. Where this was not done, a few groups found themselves in difficulties as their wax outlines faded after a few months.

In some groups there was an embroiderer who particularly enjoyed outlining, using one simple stem stitch. In other groups the outlining was shared or done by the group leader.

Stitch tension was as important here as on the work that would be seen and it could make or break the quality of the finished panel. Keeping the fabric correctly tensioned on the embroidery frame was an important aid to tensioning stitches correctly, but both were a challenge to those

A workshop with the Westminster group, with their panel mounted and tensioned on its frame.

embroiderers who had never before worked on big embroidery frames.

Some found this particularly difficult. Hilda Jenks, of Selly Oak meeting, who led the group that embroidered *Elizabeth Fry*, E5, commented: 'We enjoyed working on the woollen fabric with pleasant colours, but I, being arthritic, found working on a frame back-aching.'

Another Friend, from a different group, remembers being firmly reprimanded when she was caught by one of the teachers working her sampler without an embroidery ring. 'I'd never worked in a frame before and it seemed impossible,' she said. 'But once I understood the importance of it on these big panels I made up my mind to do it.'

Some embroiderers specialised in particular stitches, especially lettering, and on many panels this was done either by one embroiderer or by two, one of whom worked the upper case letters and the other the lower case letters.

A lettering Friend from the Harrow group, which embroidered *James Parnell; Meeting for Sufferings*, A3, recalls how the group overcame unexpected difficulties: 'When both Janet Sewell and Norah Lucas, our original enthusiast and leader, moved away, the small group of three embroiderers felt overwhelmed by the magnitude of the task. But Margaret Neill quietly continued stitching the picture, so the lettering Friends, Margaret Young and Barbara Lane, took renewed heart and the tapestry commuted between upper and lower case Friends.'

The Friend responsible for lettering on another panel points to the one word she did not embroider – it was worked by one of the embroidery teachers – and it is at once possible to see the difference, though few would notice without having their attention drawn to it. 'I see it every time I look at the panel,' she says. 'I didn't feel I should take it out and re-do it at the time, but I wish now I had.'

A member of the Oxford group, which embroidered *Persecution in Oxford*, D3, says: 'A photograph of our panel hangs in the entrance hall of the meeting house. Each time I look at it, I particularly notice one letter, a 'w', which I unpicked five times before getting it right.'

Sidmouth group, which embroidered *John Bright*, B3, received the panel ready to embroider, with the design already transferred to the calico and attached to the wool cloth. After they had completed the lettering at the bottom they were visited by Ann Castle, who found that the spacing between letters and between lines looked wrong, a fault on the original transfer. The whole section had to come out and be worked again – all 140 letters.

A Friend who saw the tapestry for the first time at an exhibition at a residential yearly meeting in Exeter was entranced by it. 'I had never sewn before and have vowed never to sew again,' she said. 'But I found the lettering very exciting. I am a legal executive and spend 80 per cent of my time divorcing people. It was good to put stitches on the *Marriage* panel.'

She subsequently became a staunch supporter of the tapestry, giving legal advice from time to time as well as being involved in mounting exhibitions.

Work was usually shared according to ability and to preference and most embroiderers seem to have managed to work on bits of their panel they particularly liked.

A member of the Salisbury group, which embroidered *William Allen*, E12, particularly enjoyed working the agricultural corner, working out stitches for cabbages, cauliflowers and hedges, while another loved embroidering gold rimmed spectacles on one of the characters and found the challenges of the more complex areas of the embroidery exciting.

'The embroidered retort came out several times. It was very difficult finding a way to make it light and glassy,' she said.

This was another very enthusiastic and happy group: 'I loved the feel of the wool, I prefer it to silks and cottons,' said one member. 'Sometimes I took the panel home, but we really enjoyed working together better.'

A scene from Quaker theatre group The Leaveners' production of Fires of Lavana *used by the Forest Hill group to guide them in embroidering* Leaveners, *C11.*

Another Friend added: 'As we worked we found the panel much more magnificent than we had imagined. We learned about embroidery, but, more importantly, we learned about the members of our meeting.'

Other groups echo this theme. 'The six of us who worked together were sorry when we had finished. We had a great feeling of fellowship together,' said a member of the Jordans group, which embroidered *Margaret Fell*, C2.

Margaret Ainger, leader of the Oxford group, remembers: 'We were aware of a gently growing friendship, particularly with a newcomer to the meeting who was a skilled embroiderer.'

Judy Quick, leader of the Gloucester & Nailsworth monthly meeting group that designed and embroidered *Work camps*, F15, says their panel was very much a monthly meeting venture, with about fifty people taking part. Her daughter came home from America to be married while embroidery was in progress and she, her husband and her husband's mother and father all embroidered apples on the tree in the bottom section.

Cathy Spence, who first came to the tapestry as a member of the Westminster group that embroidered *Mary Hughes*, E9, and subsequently went on to lead the Forest Hill group that embroidered *Leaveners*, C11, and to help with teaching, recalls how working on the tapestry helped her learn a valuable lesson.

'I'd never worked on a group project before. With this I had to share, which was difficult to begin with. Now I can't remember exactly what I did do, which is a good thing. But I do remember I had my eye on a hat. The panel went off to an exhibition and I was very disappointed when it came back embroidered by a stranger.'

The way in which work was shared out varied from group to group. Some, such as Southampton, (*Mary Fisher*, B2) divided the work at the start. 'We have each adopted a section and are trying to complete it,' wrote group leader Margaret Matthews. 'We have a file in which we write down all the decisions about colour etc.'

Rachel Abbott, of the Sevenoaks group, which embroidered *The Penn and Meade trial 1670*, F2, recorded a great deal of preparation by members of the group, who attended workshops and embroidered samplers while they waited for their panel. 'We were all very hesitant about starting the actual embroidery, but as we gained confidence we all found there were bits we could do. I avoided hair, faces and lace – but in the end found myself doing all of these, even hands.'

This was another group with upper and lower case Friends, both of whom also worked on pictures. One of them records the group's frustration when they found they were putting the wrong sort of wigs on the judges. They all had to be unpicked and reworked.

North Wales group, which embroidered *Dolgellau*

A delightful drawing (left) by a child from Mid-Somerset monthly meeting group, used on Criminal justice, E4 *(right).*

and Pennsylvania, F13, met once a week and worked together in their meeting house, two on the panel and the others doing preparation work, such as sorting colours and making samplers of sections still to be done.

'We were always very clear at the end of a Tuesday session that the panel was being given to somebody and that they should return next week having reached a certain stage. If anything happened so that they couldn't do this, there was always someone in reserve for the tapestry to go to so that we wouldn't go from one Tuesday to the next without anything being done,' says group leader Ros Morley.

Cotteridge group, which embroidered *Woodbrooke*, B6, had a similar system. 'One of the group took the tapestry home and did the bit we had discussed and agreed on. At the next meeting this was examined and sometimes had to be redone. We would then decide on the next bit and someone would offer to do it. We were a happy group with no signs of competition or adverse criticism. We just did our best and appreciated some help from Ann Castle,' said a group member.

This was one of several groups, including Sidcot (which embroidered *Friends Ambulance Unit*, F8), that embroidered panels for their own meeting houses. Cotteridge's panel, 'Quakers in industrial Birmingham', was worked as a practice panel. Friends from Sidcot designed and worked a panel

called '300 years at Sidcot' after their Quaker Tapestry panel was finished.

Mid-Somerset group met monthly with their embroidery teacher, Ann Castle, and passed their panel, *Criminal justice*, E4, from one to another in between. They were one of several groups which kept delightful little books as they worked. Theirs records, among other things, work on the coat of arms between September and November 1988: 'Another two hours . . . still plodding on . . . lion and unicorn still coming slowly, very slowly.'

The panel passed to four other embroiderers in the next few weeks until, in February 1989, the coat of arms worker recorded gleefully: 'Tom Pickles has made a frame support, which is a great help, and also found some binocular magnifying glasses – very, very helpful to me when embroidering the coat of arms, which I have just finished.'

This was one of many groups whose members took their panels to Embroiderers' Guild exhibitions. *Criminal justice* went to Wells Cathedral, where it was worked on by Hester Pickles during the Avalon Embroiderers' Guild exhibition. 'A lot of interest shown by visitors both in the work and about Quakers,' she recorded.

They also involved children, several of whom signed the book. One visit was to a Friend who wrote: 'Broke my heart to keep my resolution to spend every possible moment on the tapestry – a beautiful warm sunny day and longing to be

An example of the diagrams supplied by the teachers to embroidery groups to guide them in their use of colour.

getting on with all to do in the garden. However, hard at work on embroidery from 11.30 am. Peter Greer brought Nicola, aged four, and both whipped a line on the prison door.' Another entry, by a child, reads: 'Rowan Bullock whipped a building'.

Another Friend records collecting the tapestry and taking it to her house for the first time. 'What a terrifying responsibility. I have not embroidered since being a teenager 30 years ago. Being a direct descendant of the first Quaker to settle in my homeland, Ireland, I have been keen to try . . . I was very slow but did clothing and boots of right hand prisoner.' Her mother and brother put stitches in the Irish tapestry.

On 25 October, group leader Pamela Gould records a meeting with Ann Castle to rearrange colours in the lower section of the panel and then, horror of horrors, on 9 November, 'The wrong yellow has been used for roofs, sun and lady's top, 553 instead of 533' – and out came hours of hard work.

The way in which colour was used on panels was to a large extent outside the control of individual groups, which were given their wools and guidance on how to use the colours when they got their panels. The embroiderers then discussed the detail of their colour schemes with their teachers and sometimes made minor alterations where sections didn't work in quite the way expected. A few embroiderers went their own way, sometimes to the benefit of the whole though by no means always.

Of the 120 harmonising colours used in the Quaker Tapestry, about 30-40 were used on any one panel, chosen within the context of the panel's subject matter and the period within which the events depicted took place. In general, brighter colours could be used for events after the mid-nineteenth century, when aniline dyes were introduced.

Creative solutions

In most groups there was a core of between one and six key embroiderers who did a much bigger proportion of the work than the others, including the more difficult sections. They were also able to teach stitches and help those who wanted to put in only a few stitches.

Many of them attended at least one and often more of the residential embroidery workshops and holidays as well as workshops arranged specifically for their groups – and it was common for them to become involved in other activities such as giving talks or stewarding at exhibitions.

These were the people who were most concerned with aspects of colour and texture in the work and whose understanding of the embroidery conventions used in the Quaker Tapestry was vital.

The groups were initially issued with typed reference sheets, and later a manual, prepared by Anne Wynn-Wilson to reinforce the teachers' work. Her revised manual, *Quakers in stitches*, has since been published.

Few of the embroiderers who found the conventions of the tapestry scheme restrictive could have imagined how much difficulty Anne had in working within them, how different the Quaker Tapestry was in every way from her own work, which is strikingly contemporary and uses a wide range of techniques to develop the essence of her ideas.

On *Daniel Wheeler*, F4, designed by her and embroidered by a group in Bradford-on-Avon led by Christine Stone, her contribution literally shines out in the architecture and gleaming appliquéd gold kid domes of St Petersburg.

'None of us would have dared to do that on the Quaker Tapestry,' commented a member of the group. Probably no-one else would have dared either, except perhaps Ann Nichols, who used gold threads on a panel for the first time in the hand of God on *The voyage of the Woodhouse*, A5, embroidered by the Nottingham group.

Gold was used very sparingly on the panels and only after careful deliberation. In the case of the Woodhouse, the decision to accept a representation of the hand of God at all was not an easy one for all members of the group. Eventually, they decided that it was right to include it, as a symbol of the hope and faith displayed by the voyagers in that storm-tossed vessel, and that it should be embroidered in the form of a cloud at sunset – hence the gleam of gold.

Anne Wynn-Wilson had included the hand of God in this design to represent a blessing. 'A similar design was included in the Bayeux Tapestry, but in that case as a pointing directive,' she says.

Like Anne Wynn-Wilson, Ann Nichols is a very inventive embroiderer. She still has the first picture she worked, when she was sixteen. 'Even then I couldn't keep to the pattern,' she points out. Yet she, too, was able to accept the necessity of the disciplines of the Quaker Tapestry, gently pushing the boundaries here and there in consultation with Anne, but mainly using her inventiveness to find creative ways to solve problems.

It was she, for example, who figured out that macramé was the way to make the great chain shackling the prisoner in the *Stephen Grellet* panel, B5, and she who found a marvellous way to use the talents of a lifelong embroiderer in the Nottingham group who said she couldn't work on a panel as her sight was going and she no longer had the precision of her youth.

'We were working on the *Woodhouse* panel and we realised she might be able to do the straight stitches for the first stage of the Bayeux point on the hull of the ship,' Ann remembers. 'She still had

*Ann Nichols (left) with Margaret Rundle, Kay Cooper and
Jean Stephens of the group from Chichester and Lewes monthly
meetings which embroidered* Peace embassies, *F16.*

a wonderful colour sense – look at the colours she slipped in to make the hull look a bit grimy and seaweedy. It didn't matter if she wasn't quite precise at the ends because we came along afterwards and put in a thick Quaker stitch for those pieces that go round the hull of a ship.' The use of the stitches to develop textures is particularly striking on the *Woodhouse* panel, as it is on *Scientists*, D10, embroidered almost entirely by Winifred Booker, then of the Liskeard and Looe group. It can also be seen clearly on the first panels embroidered by Anne Wynn-Wilson while she was developing the tapestry style.

All the stitches are in the first panel, *George Fox's convincement*, A1, says Anne. Even her new stitch, Quaker stitch, is in one of the lines on Fox's clothing, though she had not recognised its value for lettering at that stage. On his sleeves she has experimented with two different methods of showing light and shade in Bayeux point, changing the colour on the left and the direction of the stitching on the right. The latter became standard practice on the tapestry.

On the second panel Anne embroidered, *Firbank Fell: George Fox preaching*, B1, the creative possibilities of these simple stitches become really clear in the central figure. 'If you look at the hair and the trousers, they are both exactly the same technique,' she points out, 'though the trousers don't look like hair or the hair like trousers.

'It's again laying the bottom threads exactly as for Bayeux, but then, if you want to be creative, you don't lay the top threads vertically or horizontally, you use a different stitch creatively to describe what you want to describe.'

The two panels also illustrate the development of the lettering technique. On the first, *George Fox's convincement*, the upper case lettering is in Anne's original style and embroidered in chain stitch. The second, *Firbank Fell*, uses Joe McCrum's new upper case alphabet, specially designed for the tapestry, for which Anne here used split stitch to try to reflect the refinement in the lettering. From then on Quaker stitch was used for lettering.

The groups were instructed carefully in how to build up a picture: background before foreground, dress people in the order that they would normally dress, outer clothes after shirts, shoes after stockings, tree trunks before branches and leaves, walls before roofs, so that the layers of embroidery would build up naturally.

Colours and textures were to be used thoughtfully, with an eye to whether they would bring elements of the picture forward or send them back. Conventions that had been established for the Quaker Tapestry to give a sense of wholeness were to be observed.

Faces and buildings were to be in outline, which was a severe test for Rugby Friends, who embroidered *World Conference 1991*, F18, and groups such as Hampstead and South Africa (*South Africa*, F19) and Chichester and Lewes (*Peace embassies*, F16), which needed to establish a range of nationalities. Suggestions of national dress often helped where it was necessary to distinguish colour or nationality.

Anne Wynn-Wilson's guidelines for the Quaker Tapestry were both a structural necessity for such a scheme and, as she had hoped, a starting point on which to base creative work, ever renewed and

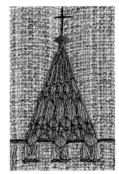

Examples from panel A1 of how chain stitch can be used: simply on the mother's skirt and father's socks, and creatively on the sheep and the church spire.

transformed by herself and others as the tapestry developed.

Outlining for buildings was a convention pushed to the limit by Ann Nichols and the Wokingham group on *Ecology*, D12, Maggie Goodrich and the Epsom group on *Friends Provident Institution*, E11, and the Netherlands group on *The Netherlands 1940-45*, F22, all of whom produced stunning buildings with considerable infill.

Swarthmoor Hall, C1, shows both interior and exterior on different parts of the same building. On *Keeping the meeting*, C3, embroidered by the Reading group, Friends are pictured holding their meeting in the brick rubble of Horsleydown meeting house in Southwark. The building had been pulled down by order of the king's surveyor, Christopher Wren.

The roof of the House of Lords in *John Bellers*, E2, embroidered by Daphne Boothby and the Hammersmith group and the stone sets in *Adult schools*, E7, embroidered by the Northampton & Wellingborough monthly meeting group are examples of convincing stonework that conformed to the convention.

Crowd scenes, trees, animals, people, ships, ironwork – the list seems endless and the variety of solutions revealed by a close study of the tapestries quite astonishing.

It's almost possible to warm the hands at the range in *Swarthmoor Hall*, C1, while the water in *George Fox at Ulverston: healing*, E1, and *Nantucket*

and Milford Haven, F12 (in each case the section embroidered by Wendy Gillett, their designer) has an extraordinary quality of wetness – strangely mirrored by the completely different approach to water in *Pilgrimages*, C9, designed and embroidered by Margaret Crosby and the north-west group.

On *Scott Bader Commonwealth*, D13, embroiderers from Northampton & Wellingborough monthly meeting were faced with challenges from the modern world: chemical drums, a tanker and industrial plant, while their children clearly enjoyed themselves on the bottom section. The modernity of the chemical industry, highlighted by the use of bright colours, contrasts strikingly with panels such as *Coalbookdale*, D4, and *Innocent trades*, D5.

Some groups were faced with unlikely challenges. The Westminster group found themselves embroidering fleas (french knots) on *Mary Hughes*, E9, while bunches of keys proved tricky for both the Sevenoaks group, F2, and Scottish Friends, A9. The lettering on the streamers on *John Bright*, B3, was particularly difficult as the streamer embroidery covered the lettering transfer.

Ann Castle, who worked the lettering on the John Bright streamers and the even more tricky lettering on the marriage certificate on *Marriage*, C8, used a jeweller's magnifying glass to help see the fine work.

Many groups went to a great deal of trouble to get the detail of their panels right. Scottish Friends went to Aberdeen and sketched the chairs and table for *Oaths*, A9, and the keys, cast in the 1690s for granting freedom of the city, that are on the table. They also photographed the portrait of Queen Anne that hangs behind and met the present provost, who showed them his halberd, the same that was in use at the time, and a portrait of the provost of the time, which enabled them to get details of his wig right.

Queen Anne appears again on *John Bellers*, E2, and was again embroidered in authentic costume after Daphne Boothby obtained permission to sketch from a portrait of her in St James's Palace. Details of the Royal coat of arms on *The Penn and Meade trial 1670*, F2, were sketched from a copy of the coat of arms in a local church.

On *George Fox: Lichfield, Pendle Hill*, D1, Anne Wynn-Wilson showed Lichfield Cathedral as George Fox would have seen it, with one of its spires smashed during the civil war.

Sometimes details were changed after panels had been completed, as in *Scientists*, D10, where a chemical formula was found to be incorrect, and *Delegation to the Czar 1854*, F5, where a railway enthusiast described the pattern of puffs of smoke that the early engine pictured would have made and they were corrected on the panel.

Bakewell and Sheffield group, which embroidered *Coalbrookdale*, D4, was one of several that used samplers to work out how to embroider various elements of their panel. The North Wales group, F13, and Jordans (*Margaret Fell*, C2) were others.

Jordans embroiderers remember practising the curls and waves for Charles II's hair, a particularly tricky part of their panel, and enjoyed working with their children, who both drew and embroidered the bottom section, which depicts the marriage of Margaret Fell and George Fox.

Margaret's six daughters, on the left, are celebrating the occasion. Her son disapproved of the match. The Jordans children, who were not impressed by his attitude, christened him 'Grumpy George' and put him to one side by himself.

Children from Colchester meeting were much involved in the design of *Children and young people*, C10, as well as the embroidery. They spent several Sunday mornings deciding what should be shown and were insistent that a wide age range be included, that children should be shown working together, that the different things that take place during the morning should be included and that they be shown taking a full part in meeting for worship.

'We were very careful about consistency,' explained one member of the group. 'The same children appeared in different places on the panel and it was important to them that they could be recognised.'

Embroidery was not easy for this group, which had a complex drawing with lots of people and found use of colour very tricky. 'It was difficult to avoid it looking bitty,' they explained. 'We had to unpick some parts four or five times and it was beginning to show on the cloth.' But, for all their ups and downs, they recorded feeling a sense of privilege in being able to take part.

Faces were a perennial difficulty. Ann Castle remembers an embroiderer who worked on the jurymen on *The Penn and Meade trial*: 'She made them all much too nice,' she says. Some groups, such as that formed by two neighbouring areas, Chichester and Lewes monthly meetings, to embroider *Peace embassies*, F16, gave all the people on their panel names and characters. This made it much easier to embroider them realistically.

Sometimes real people were depicted among the characters on panels, including *Lichfield*, D1, reproduced on the cover of this book, where faces in the crowd include embroiderers and other people Anne Wynn-Wilson knew.

Occasionally, including real people out of context could have surprising results. Anne, who would often make small changes to strengthen completed panels, added the punk figures in the front of *Quaker Peace Action Caravan*, B8, which was embroidered by the Minehead group. Several people have said they remembered seeing them when they saw Q-PAC in different parts of the country – though the figures were actually based on a young couple Anne chanced upon and spoke to one day and later thought would enliven the panel.

On *Northern Ireland: reconciliation*, F9, she added a dog, again to balance the design, and was astonished when a Friend who had been living in Quaker Cottage, Belfast, at the time the panel was embroidered arrived at an exhibition with his dog and asked her how she had known to put it in.

On a few panels, the embroiderers have added delightful details to the original designs, such as the cat in front of Winchester meeting house, embroidered by a Winchester Friend on *Meeting houses in the community*, C6, to show that the building is also someone's home, while there is a

Margaret Simpson embroidering a rose on James Nayler, *A2, watched by Celia Davies (left) and Miriam Stockbridge of the Bristol group.*

fascinating view of James Parnell's imprisonment on the bottom strip of Harrow group's panel, A3.

The children of the meeting were involved from the start, when Janet Sewell told them the story of James Parnell. 'They made a series of evocative and lively drawings,' records a member of the group. 'Stitches were practised and when Ann Nichols came to start the stitching on the panel they were confident.

'David, a scientifically minded ten-year-old, felt arrows were needed to show James Parnell falling down from a ladder and Thomas, a seven-year-old, decided the door to Colchester prison, which he stitched, should remain just a little bit open. Emma, aged six, had original ideas for the colour of the hills and wanted the wild flowers growing there to be shown too. She became so engrossed in her work she was reluctant to go home at the end of the day.'

Margaret Simpson used roses through the seasons to depict the passage of time on *James Nayler*, A2, unique among the tapestry panels in being designed as an illuminated manuscript – a fitting format for the story of an early Friend whose writings are among those most loved by many Friends. The panel was worked by the Bristol group, which later went on to mount a splendid exhibition in the city. Friends from six meetings in the Bristol area were involved and the group is notable for the tremendous amount of work its key members have done for the tapestry over the years.

They were another very happy group, with a core of skilled embroiderers in Norah Lucas, who was originally leader of the Harrow group and also took *The world family of Friends* to Switzerland; Miriam Stockbridge, who also worked on *The Underground Railroad*, F10, *George Fox at Ulverston: healing*, E1, and *True health*, D9; and Winifred Booker.

All these Friends stewarded and demonstrated at various exhibitions, and some still steward at the permanent exhibition at Kendal. Kathleen Cottrell, who masterminded the Bristol exhibition, served for some years on the Quaker Tapestry Scheme's Publications Committee, and as this book went to press, Margaret Simpson, who took on the panel for Bristol and co-ordinated the design work, was still involved in Quaker Tapestry work 16 years after her initial appointment as secretary.

Their panel was very much a group affair, with, as in all groups, a core of particularly committed workers. They enjoyed working together, with 12 people taking part in various groups and two more providing well lit working space in their homes. They also took the panel home to work on and round the meetings in the area for people to put stitches in. Margaret, who was usually far too busy with organisational work to embroider, though she is a skilled needlewoman, enjoyed embroidering the poppy on this panel.

Unusually, they had no group leader, perhaps because they had so many skilled embroiderers, and were surprised when asked how decisions about unpicking were made. They simply arranged their work between themselves and did it well.

Reaching across the world

Few embroideries can be as well travelled as the Quaker Tapestry, for while much of the embroidery was completed in the quiet of Friends' homes and meeting houses, or at exhibitions large and small, some panels travelled thousands of miles in their making.

The first to go adventuring was *Elizabeth Fry and the patchwork quilts*, E6, which Ann Castle took to Australia in 1983/84.

She had mentioned she was planning to attend Australia Yearly Meeting and visit members of her family there just as Anne Wynn-Wilson was wondering how Australian Friends could be involved in this panel – and found herself with a job to do. 'I think Anne had faith in me, but she was taking an awful risk,' she says. 'It was my first panel and it was a tremendous responsibility.'

Anne Wynn-Wilson and the Taunton children started the panel to establish the quality and style of embroidery, then the two Ann(e)s spent a day in Taunton discussing colours and use of stitches and Ann Castle started the lettering: 'That gave me a bit of confidence,' she says.

After a long, 2 am, delay at Perth customs, she was united with her anxious family. But more trials were to come. The room in which Ann was to give her talk at Australia Yearly Meeting turned out to be in a one-storey building with no form of air conditioning. The temperature was more than 100°F and the windows had to be blacked out with blankets to show the slides.

'The audience were all fanning themselves, but I couldn't as I was giving the talk. I just dripped,' Ann recorded in her diary.

But it was all worth while. Australian Friends were enthusiastic about their panel and the next day Ann found herself sitting under a gum tree in a temperature of 104°F, working on the panel and samplers with the first three Australian

embroiderers. Joyce Johnstone, an Australian Friend who was planning a trip to Britain Yearly Meeting the following year, said she would take charge of it when Ann's trip was over and bring it back to England completed.

Ann's diary records good progress in Perth, as it does as she flew on to Adelaide and Melbourne, where she notes that she managed to get four people – two adults and two children – all working on the embroidery at the same time.

She moved on to Tasmania, where Friends in Hobart learned the stitches and did some work on the panel, which inspired them to do one of their own, *Tasmania*, F20. This chronicles the work of two Quakers, James Backhouse and George Washington Walker, who tramped all over Tasmania and much of New South Wales from 1832 to 1838, enquiring into the conditions of aborigines and convicts and reporting back to Elizabeth Fry and to Parliament in London.

Back on the mainland, just outside Sydney, Ann had her fright from the wallaby, recounted on pages 7-8, which though terrifying at the time became quite a joke as she started work with Sydney Friends on the tapestry panel. This group included children from Wahroonga meeting, just outside the city, who loved working on the bottom strip. Then, after six weeks' happy travelling with the panel, it was time to go home and leave it in Joyce's care.

Both Ann(e)s were a bit apprehensive as yearly meeting approached and the panel was to be returned. It was the first panel to have been completed so far away. What would they find?

'When we opened it, it was perfect,' remembers Anne Wynn-Wilson. 'I think there were tears in all our eyes, the care that had gone into it was manifest. It was amazing.'

The Tasmania panel, designed by Martin Apstis,

*Alison Burnley (left) and Zoe Freireich working
on one of the Scottish panels at Ayr.*

was embroidered by Tasmanian Friends in 1987, under the direction of Anne Ashford of Hobart regional meeting, who was herself responsible for much of the embroidery.

Ann Castle was later to oversee *Northern Ireland: reconciliation*, F9, designed after Anne Wynn-Wilson's visit to the Family Gathering of Friends at Waterford in 1986 and embroidered by Friends in Northern Ireland.

'Almost no research was needed of the type done on the historical panels, as reconciliation was a daily fact of life for many of those involved,' said one member of the group.

Another underlined the rapport between embroiderers and their subject: 'As I worked on the panel I could visualise the visitors I had served week after week as a volunteer in the canteen at the Maze prison and tried to relate them to the figures on the tapestry.'

This much-travelled panel went back and forth from Londonderry to Richhill, with detours to Lisburn and Belfast. The first stitches were put in by an eleven-year-old girl from the meeting in Derry.

The embroiderers particularly enjoyed Anne Wynn-Wilson's visit to Dublin, the visit some of them made to a workshop in York, and Ann Castle's visits to hold workshops, which they say were highlights in the embroidery work.

Scottish Friends were equally scattered, but were used to travelling long distances to keep in touch and found all sorts of ways to move their two panels round the country.

Notes in the journals kept of making *Oaths*, A9, and *Publishers of Truth*, B4, reveal much friendship, travelling and pleasure, and include a record of Scottish Friends' own tapestry holiday – a week at Old Clachan Farmhouse, out on the west coast near Oban.

Between them the panels journeyed as far north as Orkney and south west to Newton Stewart, as well as shuttling between Glasgow, Edinburgh, Perth, Dundee, Callander and Dunblane. Sandy McEwan's account on page 7 of receiving news that the tapestry was to visit South Ronaldsay gives some idea of the joy it could bring.

Edythe Kift and her husband, Basil, travelled to this and other meetings in the north of Scotland to teach stitches and show slides. Edythe records how the Quaker Tapestry revived her interest in embroidery, which led to her embroidering samplers for each of her children 'to be family heirlooms'.

Alison Burnley of Edinburgh herself was, and is, completely entranced by the tapestry. 'I'm not an embroiderer; I sew,' she says, but her skill with people, particularly children, is memorable. She taught stitches straight on to the panels, with excellent results, and where possible recorded the names of those who embroidered even a stitch or two. Each child's name and address was recorded and when the panels were complete, she sent each one a postcard of the finished picture.

The Haida salmon from panel F21.

Similar skills, together with an excellent eye for colour and tremendous ability as an embroiderer, enabled Ann Nichols not only to enthuse many groups in this country, but also to cross a continent with the *Canada*, F21, panel. She designed this with Canadian-born Bette Dewhurst, who also designed and helped embroider *Merchants*, D6.

Canadian Friends had been asking for some time to do a panel, though workshops run by two other visiting friends, in Toronto and Vancouver, hadn't been enough to get it going. Ann and her husband, Harold, who wanted to visit their family in Canada anyway, decided to extend their trip and take a panel.

They prepared carefully. Harold corresponded with Canadian Friends in 83 meetings across Canada, asking what they wanted on the panel and whether they would like a visit so that they could embroider. Sixty replied and were again consulted about the composite ideas for design. They were happy with the design ideas and most meetings wanted visits – so the Canadian trip could take shape.

Ann and Harold started in Victoria, on Vancouver Island, and travelled north up the west coast, eventually travelling out to the Queen Charlotte Islands to visit the six Quakers there, who welcomed them warmly but asked why the salmon on the picture was not a native Haida salmon. This was soon put right by substituting a glorious drawing by Alfred Muma, after the style of Haida Indian artist Bill Reed.

At Victoria meeting, the gap left for children's drawings was filled by the children's account of their adoption of two schools in Mexico, to which they sent school equipment as Christmas presents.

One year they asked the Mexican children what they wanted and the answer was fruit trees, which were duly provided, together with expert help in planting. They are shown on the bottom of panel F21 under a hot Mexican sun. Children across Canada were told the story and added stitches to the pictures.

Friends in the Toronto/Niagara area worked on the panel while Ann and Harold took some holiday towards the end of their trip, then the almost complete panel was finished by Canadian Friends in England.

Canada also has close connections with the American panel, *The Underground Railroad*, F10, which tells the story of American Friends helping fugitive slaves to escape to safe havens in Canada during the nineteenth century.

Anne Wynn-Wilson had visited America twice, as Friends there were keen to know about the tapestry. On the first trip, she went with Ann Castle to New England Yearly Meeting, where she set up an exhibition, led three workshops and gave a main session with slides. Interest was such that Anne Wynn-Wilson was invited to return to America to teach for a term at the Quaker college at Pendle Hill.

The Armitage sisters (from left), Miriam Stockbridge, Celia Ball, and Nancy Goddard, during the Quaker Tapestry exhibition at Bayeux in 1990.

Ruth Hall Brooks with the North American Quaker Tapestry panel completed by Willistown Friends group, Pennsylvania.

This time, Margaret Simpson travelled with her. They first visited New York, where Anne gave a workshop, and then attended Philadelphia Yearly Meeting where they exhibited two panels of the tapestry. Margaret returned home after a short holiday and Anne spent a term at Pendle Hill, during which she researched and designed *The Underground Railroad* with American Friends.

She took with her *The world family of Friends*, on which American children embroidered the bottom strip, which included drawings by children from America, Brazil, Canada, Chile, Europe, and Japan.

But the American adults had become so enthusiastic that they commissioned their own fabric and, using Appletons wools, are now working on ten panels of their own. Designs for the North American Quaker Tapestry are based on the style established by Anne Wynn-Wilson and use the same lettering.

American Friends were also keen to see the original Quaker Tapestry and mounted a series of successful exhibitions in Quaker colleges in the winter of 1993/94.

The Underground Railroad was taken on by three sisters, Miriam Stockbridge, Celia Ball and Nancy Goddard, known as the Armitage sisters from their maiden name. They were born in Canada but now all live in England and were particularly keen to work on the panel as they had grown up hearing their parents' stories of the Underground Railroad.

They shared the panel with others who wanted to embroider, including a woman who had had a stroke. 'It took her about 15 minutes to do the French knot that marks the most northerly town on the map, but she was thrilled to have done

something,' says Miriam.

This is just one of many stories of the powerful need some Friends had to be part of the project. A man from the one of the embroidery groups says he is certain his wife, who had a terminal illness, stayed alive just to finish her section of their panel, while Irish Friends record that their need for an artist to work on *Ireland: The great hunger 1845-8*, E8, prompted an artist who had had a stroke to draw again and later to embroider. 'For all of us, this was the high point of our experience with the tapestry.'

In New Zealand, where tapestry teacher Brenda Meadows could see no way to help six-week-old Briony put in a stitch, her parents placed her hand on the panel and said: 'We will tell her she touched it.' Another New Zealand Friend was so elated she was able to put in a stitch that as she left she said she felt like dancing.

Brenda travelled 10,000 kilometres with *New Zealand/Aotearoa*, F14, during 1988. Her route stretched from Whangarei in the north of North Island to Dunedin on the south-east coast of South Island, with Brenda helping Friends to embroider and giving talks and broadcasts along the way.

She describes her journey as 'cementing the cause of peace' and comments on the value of the few minutes silence she would share with Friends on her travels before work started. The youngest child to put in a stitch here was three years old, as have been the youngest Scottish, English and Canadian contributors.

The *New Zealand/Aotearoa* panel's travels were funded by an English Friend with New Zealand connections, Katharine Gell, whose generosity to

Brenda Meadows demonstrating embroidery on the
New Zealand/Aotearoa *panel, F14, at Christchurch Friends*
meeting house in September 1988.

the Quaker Tapestry stretched from the start of the project to her death in 1995. She donated $10,000 NZ to cover the travelling costs of New Zealand Friends, who she realised rarely met one another. Only $5,500 NZ was used. The remainder, with her agreement, seeded a fund for a Quaker sheltered housing project in New Zealand.

Design for this panel, by Karol London, was a far simpler process than that for *South Africa*, F19, designed in England by Avril Brown, though both are concerned with the theme of working for freedom, justice and peace between races. This was a panel shared by Friends in South Africa and the Hampstead monthly meeting group in England, members of which have connections with South Africa. At the time it was being designed, much of the work of South African Friends was too sensitive to be shown, in case it damaged their contribution to bringing an end to apartheid in that country.

After much heart-searching, it was seen to be wisest to depict mainly historical events, though Olive Gibson's work with African families in Johannesburg and that of the Quaker Peace Centre in Cape Town have been included.

Behind the scenes

*An ad-hoc committee meeting during the Tapestry
exhibition at yearly meeting in Exeter, 1986.*

As the tapestry project grew, so it provided Friends
with many of the opportunities that Anne Wynn-
Wilson had originally envisaged. Friends travelled,
learned new skills, made new friends and co-
operated in a unique community project.

They also gave a tremendous amount of time and
money, and those at the centre, many of whom
were retired, worked at least as hard, if not harder,
than they had previously done in their paid
employment.

For behind the beauty of the panels and the
dedication of the embroiderers lies a miracle of
organisation by a handful of people. There would
have been no tapestry if Anne Wynn-Wilson's
vision and sense of religious calling to carry it
through had not been powerful enough to inspire a
core of helpers who supported it through thick and
thin and financed most of their own extensive
travels.

As the tapestry scheme expanded, the committee
members found themselves doing far more work

than they could possibly have expected, for while
Anne truly was an inspiration to them, she was
also a visionary, a perfectionist and a hard
taskmaster. It was not that she intended to
overstretch her helpers, but that she seemed to
assume everyone to have skills, dedication and
enthusiasm equal to her own – if only they would
allow themselves to see it.

Some had. Others found themselves close to
their limits or over-committed. Several keen
tapestry supporters were lost to the committee
because they were not, or did not wish to be, in a
position to give their all to the tapestry and accept
Anne's style of leadership. By her own admission,
this was closer to that of a managing director than
is usual in Quaker circles, though her sense of
being led by God was strong and her memory of
the first years of the committee is one of closely
gathered meetings that were able to discern the
right way forward.

The panel selection, research, design and

embroidery work described in earlier chapters was the most visible and obvious part of their work. Beneath that lay another layer of organisation without which there could not have been a tapestry on this scale.

Weekend workshops took a tremendous amount of organisation as they were on the one hand an efficient and pleasurable way of transmitting skills, but on the other a potential source of financial loss to the tapestry if they did not attract enough people – a few had to be cancelled to avoid such losses.

More work was generated by the tapestry holidays and the big exhibitions, all of which were meticulously planned and each of which involved several layers of organisation.

Anne Wynn-Wilson and Margaret Simpson were responsible for organising the first holiday, at the Quaker guest house Glenthorne, in the Lake District, and for setting up detailed arrangements for most of the big exhibitions. But much of the donkey work for visits to France, first for a memorable holiday at Charbonnières and later for the exhibition at Bayeux, was handed over to Janet Sewell and her husband, Joseph.

Janet and Joe Sewell

They organised the bookings and accommodation on both occasions and helped with other arrangements, though, as always, several members of the committee contributed, including Anne and Margaret.

For the Bayeux exhibition, which was the direct result of a meeting with the directrice of the Bayeux museum during the Charbonnières holiday, arrangements became much more complicated. Not only had stewarding and accommodation to be arranged, but also a host of domestic details, timings for press conferences, French translations of information about the tapestry and children's quiz sheets, arrangements for getting the panels and shop goods through customs, arrangements for hanging panels, and training for stewards. All this work started more than a year before the event and continued in tandem with embroidery workshops and plans for a series of major exhibitions in England, Scotland and Ireland.

Notices in the *Newsletter* and at yearly meeting asking for help with stewarding elicited an enormous response. Everyone, it seemed, wanted to be part of the tapestry's visit to Bayeux. The Sewells were characteristically businesslike in their approach to selecting helpers. They needed people with language skills and embroidery skills, car drivers, people able to handle cash for tapestry sales and, just as importantly, people who would be reliable and get on with one another.

Many applicants were inevitably disappointed, including Friends who had been strong supporters of the tapestry from the start, but the Sewells' success may be gauged by the fact that everyone who had agreed to turn up did so, stewarding was friendly and efficient, and memories of their time at Bayeux are among the happiest for many tapestry supporters.

Accommodation for a holiday in Bayeux for those not on the stewarding rota was arranged by Ann Cuming. Ann embroidered on Scottish panels and later developed a delightful garden at Kendal meeting house, where visitors to the exhibition can see many of the plants associated with Quaker botanists, including some of those shown on *Botanists*, D8, worked by the embroidery teachers.

Invitations to join this were sent out with letters to those not chosen to steward and it proved a successful alternative for many, while others joined a Quaker Camp arranged independently by Kurt and Ann Strauss at Creully, 14 km from Bayeux.

Holidays and workshops were a happy and successful part of the Quaker Tapestry experience, but they were also the icing on what became a very substantial cake.

For the tapestry committee was not just about embroideries. Fund-raising was a crucial part of its work from the start. Subscriptions from the membership group organised by Margaret Simpson, which in the first year totalled £359, rose steadily to £2,861 by 1993, leaping to £4,864 in 1994 after the introduction of life membership and hitting a high of £7,916 in 1995 during the fund-raising drive to house and exhibit the Tapestry at Kendal.

Donations, some anonymous, also provided a useful income, peaking in 1989/90 at £10,773 after

*Life after the Tapestry for Pamela
and Arthur Harrison.*

an appeal to underwrite exhibition costs. Appeals to trusts raised some money. Hire fees for the use of panels in exhibitions, introduced in 1991, brought in another £14,000 over four years.

But the star performer turned out to be sales of goods. The notelets and embroidery kits, initially made by Anne and Friends from Taunton and sold by Peggy Sumption, brought in £417 in the first year, almost half the tapestry's income. The sales gradually developed into what became known as the Tapestry Market, which generated a considerable cash flow over the years.

Soon after Anne had moved from Taunton to Bradford-on-Avon, Peggy indicated she would like to stand down as market manager and she was replaced in 1986 by Pamela Harrison, of Wokingham, who was to serve for eight years. 'We drove down to Margaret Simpson's house in Bristol and collected a few things from Peggy in the boot of the car,' Pamela remembers. 'It really seemed quite a simple job.'

What she had not expected was to find herself and her husband, Arthur, immediately co-opted onto the tapestry committee and involved in a sales drive. 'I was perfectly happy to receive orders, send out goods and keep the books straight,' she remembers, 'but I really didn't know anything about stock and marketing and what might sell, though I had a few ideas later on.'

Anne Wynn-Wilson was still bursting with ideas, including the hugely successful tapestry calendars,

which in theory could generate a profit of up to 100 per cent – providing print runs were pitched at the right level. The first, which was underwritten by personal loans from committee members, sold out very quickly and went into a second printing. Later, it became more difficult to predict quantities accurately, especially as sales were so seasonal.

Paid-up members of the tapestry supporters scheme have received free calendars from the start and a discount arrangement encourages them to sell calendars in their meetings.

Market goods have included sewing kits, stitch guides, notelets, notepaper, postcards (eventually one of each panel), greetings cards, slides, table mats and coasters, and, from 1990, books, guides to the panels and posters.

The first year's calendar sales almost doubled net income from the Tapestry Market, from £2,770 in year ending March 1986 to £5,080 in the following year. Net income from the market fluctuated between £4,200 and £5,300 for the next three years, shooting up to £21,000 in 1991, when Ormerod Greenwood's book *The Quaker Tapestry* was published and income from the travelling exhibitions and the big exhibitions in Aberdeen, London and Bayeux began to feed through. The Festival Hall exhibition alone took £16,621. At this stage sales generated some two thirds of gross income for the tapestry.

The average for 1992 and 1993 was similar, while exhibitions were still on the road, then income fell sharply as the number of big travelling exhibitions declined and the panels were recalled to prepare for the permanent exhibition at Kendal.

During the heyday of travelling exhibitions, many of which generated turnovers of £2,000 or more in sales, the Tapestry Market became big business for a small charity. It often took Pamela all morning every day to pack up the orders, which then had to be taken to the post office and stamped, a heavy and time-consuming task – especially if Arthur happened to be away and she had to carry everything in her shopping trolley.

She had hoped to lay the task down in September 1990, but no replacement could be found, so she agreed to continue until the shop goods were handed over to help stock the shop at the Kendal exhibition.

Arthur had proved to be a marvellous find for the committee. The tapestry was also a very satisfactory niche for Arthur in the Religious Society of Friends. 'Most Friends are academics and much of the society's work tends to be intellectual, but here was a place where practical skills were valued,' he said – a sentiment echoed by several embroiderers.

He was soon hard at work making the plywood boards on which the completed panels were mounted and boxes in which they could be transported when people wanted to borrow them for exhibitions or demonstrations.

Later on, the question of wear and tear on the panels had to be addressed and it was decided that the panels should be attached to backing boards bigger than themselves that would act as frames and enable them to be handled and exhibited without being touched.

These were made of hardboard, which had to be treated with a special chemical to seal it and prevent acids from the board damaging the tapestry fabric. 'The fumes were terrible,' says Arthur, 'I had to wear a mask and gloves to handle it.'

Yet in his tiny workshop in a shed at the bottom of his garden, Arthur has made and treated hundreds of these boards as well as sufficient boxes to transport all the panels. 'When photographic reproductions of panels came in they all had to have backing boards as well,' he says.

Soon he and Pamela began to store completed panels, releasing them for loan as required. 'We rented a garage to store shop stock, as there soon wasn't room in the house for it all, and the panels were stored there as well,' he explains. 'When the travelling exhibitions began, I was asked to buy a trailer and then I travelled all over the country with panels. I hung most of the big exhibitions too.'

Panel storage was transferred in September 1990 to a house in the Cotswolds and later to Ray Noyce's house in Derbyshire, though Arthur continued to help hang exhibitions until the Kendal exhibition opened.

For Pamela and Arthur, as for most of the Friends closely involved with the Quaker Tapestry, the friendships they made through the work and their appreciation of the value of the project far outweighed the inconvenience of periods of sheer exhaustion. Pamela still stewards at Kendal, though Arthur has now found a new outlet for his practical abilities – building working scale models of steam engines.

In the early years, the tapestry committee was much concerned with establishing its status within the Society of Friends, and thus its position in terms of fund-raising. Anne Wynn-Wilson's hopes that it could be officially part of Children & Young People's Committee were eventually dashed and between 1984 and 1986 Margaret and other members of the Tapestry committee were involved in drawing up a constitution to ensure registration as a charity.

This both gave the Quaker Tapestry Scheme independence and enabled the treasurers, first Henry Rowntree, then, from 1986, Noel Cliffe, and from 1991 until 1998 Ray Noyce, to appeal more widely for funding.

Margaret was later involved in ensuring that the Quaker Tapestry Scheme's copyright over reproduction of its panels was secure, so that it could exercise protection and control. This became increasingly important as panels went on public exhibition and Friends became involved in television programmes and newspaper and magazine coverage. Christine Davis, one of the driving forces behind the Scottish panels, made a series of six television programmes for *Late Call*, a Scottish religious programme; Anne Wynn-Wilson made a series with Forge Productions for transmission by the BBC; and others included programmes for Tyne Tees, ITV, and at least one in Welsh, sparked by publicity material for an exhibition.

Exhibition publicity also generated extensive coverage on local radio and in newspapers, while several articles have appeared in women's and

Christine Davis (left) and Alison Burnley with their embroidery frame and a box made to transport it in. After completion of the Scottish panels they joined a group in making this Peace panel.

embroidery magazines over the years.

Friends across the country gave – and still give – talks and slide shows, an art that perhaps reaches its peak with Alison Burnley and Christine Davis in Scotland. They have been among the most active promoters of the tapestry from the start and have spoken to just about every kind of group imaginable from Rotaries to Women's Institutes.

'We'll go to anyone, anywhere, who will have us,' says Alison, delighting in the wholly unexpected discovery that she has an aptitude for selling things. 'Christine does most of the talking and I drive and set up a sales table. It's a marvellous way of spreading the word about Quakers and raising funds and I love it.'

Publications played an increasingly important role with the production first of exhibition catalogues and children's worksheets, then, in 1992, of the first *Guide in colour*, an enormous undertaking that involved re-photographing every panel to get consistency of colour.

An education pack was published and a series of four booklets that enlarged on the subjects of individual panels, including *Quaker marriage* and *Quaker meeting houses*. A 'Bedside Book' was envisaged, for which Betty Harris did a tremendous amount of research. It was never published, but her work later provided a marvellous foundation for the research for this book and the Quaker Tapestry archives.

Although six sub-committees had been formed in 1986 to simplify the committee's workload, most members were on at least three of these and Anne Wynn-Wilson had a hand in almost everything. Correspondence and design back-logs piled up, the number of panels crept up to 77, attempts to give her secretarial help consistently failed, ideas that needed other people's energy and/or money flowed incessantly and some Friends began to feel that too many unilateral decisions were being made.

Conversely, Anne, whose creative drive was in top gear, was constantly frustrated by what she saw as other people's lack of vision as idea after idea was lost or not carried through. But she needed her helpers and they were captivated by the tapestry and steadfastly loyal to its creator.

Those who had worked hardest and longest for the tapestry, the three Ann(e)s, Margaret Simpson and Harold Nichols, saw it through the big exhibitions in 1989 and 1990. But there followed a parting of the ways.

Ann and Harold Nichols resigned from the committee, though Ann has since maintained close links with the tapestry, helped Anne Wynn-Wilson see the last few panels through to completion and continues to give considerable help at Kendal. Ann Castle, by then 78 years old, retired from the committee but continues to demonstrate at exhibitions in the south.

The committee would clearly have a new function and needed a new structure. Edward Milligan, an experienced clerk and great supporter of the tapestry, was asked to clerk it as it moved into a period of consolidation, during which the emphasis was on publications, organising exhibitions, building up funds for a permanent exhibition and setting up the legal and organisational framework for the Kendal exhibition.

Some new members were appointed to the committee and continuity was provided by others, including Margaret Simpson, Janet Sewell, and treasurer Noel Cliffe, remaining in place.

Anne Wynn-Wilson continued to serve briefly. She resigned in 1991, but continued with design and oversight for the remaining panels. She was also involved in setting up the permanent exhibition at Kendal and became one of its first trustees.

On the road

It was not just panels in the making that travelled, completed panels were often on display almost as soon as they could be mounted, though exhibitions on the grand scale were not part of Anne Wynn-Wilson's original vision.

Her early correspondence with Quaker Home Service in July 1981 speaks of a much simpler project, where children would be told stories which they would interpret in drawings and written work. A central co-ordinator would make selections from this work to translate into a working drawing for embroidery, which would then be completed by the children with help from adults.

But once the first panel had been completed and displayed as part of Anne's presentation of the tapestry scheme at yearly meeting at Warwick in 1982 it rapidly became clear both that the scheme would develop very differently and that the panels were to be embroidered to exhibition standard.

The final minute of the newly formed committee reads: 'It was intended there should be a small exhibition at each yearly meeting and a larger one at the next residential meeting in four years' time. It was hoped the completed work would be exhibited at a yearly meeting in eight years' time.'

The million dollar question, raised then and throughout the embroidery project but not to be resolved for another ten years, was 'what will be done with the panels when they are finished?'

Those who took part in the scheme did so in faith, though Anne and the committee were always on the lookout for a final home for the tapestries.

Many of those who did not take part were concerned not just about the cost of the scheme itself but also the possibility that the embroiderers were creating a future practical and financial liability for the Religious Society of Friends.

By the time the Quaker Tapestry Scheme became a separate charity in August 1986 its own aims were clear. It was to 'advance religion according to the principles and practices of the Religious Society of Friends by exploring arts and crafts such as embroidery by the production of an embroidered hanging depicting the story of the people known as Quakers'. It was also 'to advance education by extending knowledge of Quakerism within and beyond the Religious Society of Friends by creating and using the Quaker Tapestry'.

The constitution included powers to 'hold and participate in exhibitions in any part of the world' and to 'lend the Quaker Tapestry to exhibitions, subject to availability, provided the borrowers accept responsibility for its safe keeping, for collecting and returning it, for handling it with special care, and to charge a reasonable rate for the lending'.

There was no answer to the million-dollar question because no-one had one. Members of the tapestry scheme had taken responsibility for the time being, though the last paragraph of the constitution makes disturbing reading for the Jeremiahs: 'If the organisation ceases to exist or it shall be decided by resolution at any Annual General or Extraordinary General Meeting to wind it up, the net assets after payment of all liabilities and the finished Quaker Tapestry shall be transferred to Meeting for Sufferings of London Yearly Meeting of the Religious Society of Friends or its successor body.'

But the last thing the committee wanted to consider was the possibility of the Tapestry Scheme ceasing to exist. Its independence simply enabled it to get on with its work without reference to official Quaker organisation – and it did.

The first *George Fox* panel, A1, was soon on public display, when Sutton meeting borrowed it in the summer of 1983 to form part of an exhibition in their local library on Quakerism. In August of

The Mayor of Bayeux putting a stitch in the Tapestry.

the same year, the next panel to be completed, *Firbank Fell: George Fox preaching*, B1, was displayed in the annual exhibition of the Devon Guild of Craftsmen at Totnes.

During the next few years, as the scheme became more widely known, panels continued to be in demand for small local exhibitions. In 1987 it was reported that there was 'a great demand to borrow tapestry panels to accompany *Meet the Quakers* exhibitions in meeting houses, some had been lent to Hemel Hempstead meeting for a peace exhibition, an exhibition including photographic copies of panels was on its way to a family gathering in East Germany, and another had been left in France for their yearly meeting'.

Ann Castle had put on a small exhibition to raise funds for the tapestry, an example followed by several other tapestry supporters over the years, and each year until 1993, the committee organised an exhibition at yearly meeting, soon establishing a hold on a landing at Friends House to which they returned year after year.

As demand for exhibitions grew and more panels became available, it became necessary to organise loans more carefully. In 1986, the committee noted concerns over transport and security and Harold Nichols was asked to prepare a procedure for lending panels for exhibition. Arthur Harrison, who had made a box for transporting panels, was asked to make more, with space for shop goods to be sold at exhibitions.

By this time there were also sets of slides available that could be used by people giving talks, which opened up the possibility utilised by

Wokingham meeting of holding a Quaker exhibition at their meeting house, including all the completed panels and a talk with slides by Ann Nichols.

This combination of exhibitions and talks became a very successful format, with some meetings, such as Newcastle upon Tyne, also managing to secure television and radio coverage. Members of Embroiderers' Guild groups are among those who still request talks and slide shows from time to time and have been regular visitors to tapestry exhibitions over the years.

Since early 1984, completed panels had been insured, but such valuations are always to some extent arbitrary and to those who borrowed or transported panels, it was their intrinsic value as irreplaceable examples of community work that was uppermost – and there were one or two nasty moments.

Anne Wynn-Wilson recalls that she and Margaret Simpson had to stand helplessly by when a car caught fire in a field at an exhibition. It was parked close to the one in which they were carrying completed panels and other materials for demonstrations. 'We weren't allowed to go near it, or to rescue anything or to drive it away. Fortunately the fire engine came very, very quickly, but it was a very tense nine minutes.'

Another Friend had to go through the process of exchanging insurance details with a driver who had crashed into the back of her car while she was carrying completed panels in the boot. 'All I wanted to do was open the boot and see if the panels were alright,' she remembers. They were, as was the one left propped by the booking office on a railway station by a Friend rushing to catch a train.

'It was about to pull out when I found I hadn't got the panel,' she says. 'The train waited while I rushed back to get it – but I was not able to tell my group leader until years later.'

Conservationists at the Victoria & Albert Museum had advised that no panel should be exhibited more than three times a year if deterioration was to be avoided. On the other hand, the constitution of the Quaker Tapestry Scheme specifically refers to using the tapestry to extend knowledge of Quakerism within and beyond the Society of Friends.

The compromise reached was to satisfy the demand for exhibitions in the short term, to develop high quality photographic reproductions that could be used for travelling exhibitions in the

Listen, look or put in a stitch: the Tapestry exhibition in Central Edinburgh meeting house during August 1989.

Walter Miller (left) and Ron Halliday, clerks of the two Quaker meetings in Edingburgh working on Oaths, A9.

longer term, and to tighten up security and care arrangements where real panels were exhibited.

Real panels, changed from time to time, went on permanent display in three Quaker centres, Charney Manor, William Penn House in London and Swarthmoor Hall, and from 1987 forwards one real panel was included with photographs for small exhibitions.

The annual exhibitions at yearly meetings continued to attract attention and by 1987 a booking had been made for a major exhibition in Aberdeen Art Gallery from 29 July to 12 August 1989 to coincide with a residential yearly meeting in the city and projected completion of the Quaker Tapestry. It was to move on to Central Edinburgh meeting, where all the panels would be exhibited in the meeting house during the Edinburgh Festival.

Arrangements were also in hand for the exhibition in Bayeux in 1990, in the same building as the Bayeux Tapestry. An exhibition was arranged for a month in the spring of 1990 at the Royal Festival Hall in London.

The opening of this exhibition was to coincide with a performance of a choral drama celebrating the integrity of creation, *Cry of the earth*, performed in the Festival Hall by The Quaker Festival Orchestra & Chorus (see panel C11).

In the early stages of planning, the committee saw an exhibition in Nottingham as a dress rehearsal for their first major display to the public in Aberdeen Art Gallery. But in the end it was cancelled. There was simply too much to do.

As always, the committee planned these events meticulously. Several visits were made to each venue to plan hanging, arrangements for tapestry market sales, security, accommodation, and a host of other details. Stewards had to be found, rotas made and training given. Catalogues had to be prepared and, in the run-up to the Festival Hall exhibition, a major crisis had to be averted when Ormerod Greenwood died, leaving much work to be done before his book, *The Quaker Tapestry*, could be published.

Edward Milligan and his sister Mary generously stepped in to complete the manuscript, working hectically to meet an imminent deadline. The first edition soon sold out following its Festival Hall launch.

Between the first big public exhibition of all completed panels, which opened on 29 July 1989, and the opening of the permanent exhibition in Kendal on 25 April 1994, panels travelled all over Britain and Ireland, to France and to five States in North America.

Venues ranged from Quaker meeting houses to churches, from art galleries to museums, from public libraries to stately homes. Panels were also displayed in 1992, 1993 and 1995 at the annual Needlecraft Fair in London.

In all, there were almost 100 exhibitions during this time. Each had to be organised, hung and stewarded. The right panels had to be despatched and appropriate leaflets and labels made. To ensure an exhibition's success, good publicity was vital. Local schools, embroiderers' groups, newspapers, television and radio needed to be invited in good time and an opening ceremony could increase publicity and swell attendance. Where possible, Tapestry Market goods were on sale.

Even for small exhibitions planning normally

*The Quaker Tapestry exhibition at the House
of Commons in March 1991.*

started at least a year beforehand and the Quaker Tapestry Scheme committee prepared an excellent series of guidelines for exhibitors, regularly updated in the light of experience.

Anne Wynn-Wilson, although no longer on the committee for most of this period, helped plan the hanging sequences for many of the bigger exhibitions. Particularly successful ones were held at St Albans Abbey (1991), Bristol (1991), Belfast (1992), Dublin (1992), and Glasgow (1993). Arthur Harrison and/or Ray Noyce were often on hand to hang them and, when possible, Anne would stay to demonstrate embroidery. Each exhibition also needed a printed guide, for which Margaret Simpson supplied information.

Since the opening of the exhibition at Kendal, a series of small exhibitions of full-size photographic reproductions have continued their travels, together with one or two real panels where security is sufficiently good and panels can be spared. A marvellous exhibition of all the completed panels was mounted in Winchester Cathedral in February 1996 and others are booked for Canterbury and Rochester Cathedrals in February 1999.

A work of love

The Quaker Tapestry exhibitions were and are just magical, a celebration of years of work by thousands of people across the world and a revelation both to the participants and to those who see the embroideries for the first time.

The panels speak to different people in different ways and almost all exhibition organisers and stewards have stories of visitors who returned two or three times, visibly moved and sometimes needing to share their experiences.

Sometimes these are very specific, as with the visitor to the Kendal exhibition who told of a previous visit with members of her family. They were facing family difficulties and had not been able to see how to go forward. 'But after we came out of the exhibition, something had happened. We could all see what to do and peace was restored,' she said. On her second visit, she was feeling a sense of loss. The panels no longer seemed to speak to her so powerfully.

Another young woman, whose quest for spiritual solace following the death of her father was proving frustratingly barren, happened upon the tapestry exhibition at Bradford Museum in 1991. For her it was the starting point of a spiritual journey that in time was to lead to her attending meetings for worship, joining the Religious Society of Friends, and eventually playing a leading role in founding a new meeting when she moved to a town without one.

The power of the tapestry stayed with her. As are so many visitors to the exhibitions, she was amazed by the number of 'pretty good' historical figures who were Quaker. 'How could all these people possibly be of one tradition?' she asked. But it was the power of the embroideries themselves that made the deepest impression.

'The quality of stitching is so sublime. It isn't so much to do with the sheer perfection of it, but to do with how it was done. I could feel the people who had done it,' she says.

'Then I started to read what was said on some of the panels and this really got to me. But as far as I knew I didn't know any living Quakers, so I thought "there's no way I'm joining a funny closed sect". And there it sat for six months or so.'

During this time she read widely and felt drawn back to her church roots, 'even if not in a strictly orthodox Christian way', but found she was no longer able to attend church services. 'It was meaningless, compared to what I had been thinking,' she explains. 'I didn't want to be spoon fed by a vicar any longer.'

This woman's twentieth-century search for 'truth' was soon to be rewarded. She discovered that a colleague in a string quartet in which she played was a Quaker. A woman she had always liked was one of these 'weird people'. She turned down an invitation to meeting for worship but was happy to borrow books. Then a tapestry exhibition was mounted in Watford, her home town, and she was hooked.

'I just stood in there, marvelling, and thought "you can't waste time any longer" and went to meeting the next Sunday.'

Others have come to Friends' meetings through contact with the tapestry, though exhibitors hoping for instant rejuvenation of their meetings are likely to be disappointed. Much more rewarding for them are the touching and amusing contacts with visitors.

'The jeans-clad mayor blew in and wanted to buy the *Meeting houses overseas* panel on the spot,' says a Friend's account of a small exhibition in the French town of Congénies. The enthusiastic young Frenchman was eventually given a reproduction of the panel by French and English Friends, who had much enjoyed a week's stay in the town.

While few respond quite so dramatically, it is not

uncommon for visitors to relate their connections with panels. 'One morning a Londoner approached us, telling us she had known Mary Hughes of Whitechapel,' recalls Edythe Kift in an account of her week's stewarding at Bayeux. 'She had lived as a child quite near the Dewdrop Inn and in particular recalled the incident portrayed on the bottom strip, where Mary, leading a march of unemployed people, was knocked down by a tram: she accepted all the blame for the accident herself, declaring the driver was not in any way responsible.'

Another steward at the Bayeux exhibition remembers children happily filling in questionnaires asking them how many ducks, chickens and frogs they could find in the panels. 'This was an inspired activity someone before us had devised,' she says.

Her two-page account of the pleasures of her week at Bayeux conclude: 'I should end by confessing that when the tapestry was first brought to our attention at yearly meeting, I was one of those Friends who thought it a pleasant activity but couldn't see much point . . . how salutary, and how satisfying, to have been proved to be so completely mistaken. I think it is one of the greatest pieces of extension work this century and am most grateful to have been allowed a small part in it.'

Highlights of the exhibition at Haverford West, in Wales, included a visit from David Folger, a descendant of one of the original Quaker settlers in the town, who brought his wife and two daughters over from New England especially for the event. The organisers also had a pleasant surprise when they went to collect their trailer full of panels, which had been shipped over from a previous exhibition at Waterford, Ireland. They were waved through customs without the usual thorough search goods from that country were normally accorded in 1992. 'It seems Quakers are still seen as people to be trusted,' they said.

Some attempts to attract school parties to exhibitions were more successful than others. A teacher who took two classes to the Dublin exhibition after a Friend had given a talk in her school was impressed by the way the tapestry captured the imagination of young and old. Six months after the exhibition her pupils were able to recall vividly many of the stories and events depicted and were able to remember particular Quaker messages from some of the panels.

Children from Kingshill School, Cirencester, wrote about their visit to an exhibition in the town in 1990. They were clearly impressed, but many considered Quaker values idealistic rather than realistic. One pupil's account includes: 'When I looked at the first panel I noticed the brilliant craftsmanship . . . the clothes and hair actually stood out on the fabric. One flower took nine hours to sew. This shows the same sort of dedication they have shown in their principles and beliefs.'

He also included comments on beliefs, such as: ' "We utterly deny all outward war and strife and fighting with outward weapons, for any end whatever . . . . this is our testimony to the world." This statement includes self defence. I personally think it is not humanly possible to stand there and be killed or beaten and not fight back. But in principle this belief is a good concept. If the whole world thought this a lot of suffering would stop.'

The very successful exhibition at Strathclyde Museum of Education, a stunning building in Glasgow designed by Charles Rennie Mackintosh, attracted 6,275 visitors in four weeks, a record for the museum. 'Joy was what was seen time and time again on the faces of our visitors,' reported organiser Jenny Auld. Not every visitor signed the visitors' book, but nearly all who did were complimentary – apart from the odd, very odd, boy who wrote 'boring'!

'There was one magnificent surprise which sums up all my feelings about the exhibition. When he had left, we found a young Russian man from Moscow had written: "Thank you for so warm an exhibition".'

A meeting between Anne Wynn-Wilson and a Friend from Kendal in 1991 was to open the door to a permanent exhibition centre in the heart of what is known to Quakers as '1652 country', the area in which Quakerism was born.

Here, in the Lake District, a permanent exhibition has been set up in part of the town's meeting house, a beautiful Grade II listed building that is far too big for the existing meeting. A joint agreement has allowed the building to be shared by the Quaker Tapestry and Kendal Friends.

The exhibition, which has space to display the complete tapestry, was designed by Andrew James, a Nottingham Friend and director of the Museum of Nottingham Lace, in consultation with Anne Wynn-Wilson. Here again, the conflict between conservation and display has been resolved in

Rachel Abbott working beneath an exhibition at Kendal of children's panels inspired by the Quaker Tapestry.

Ann Cuming in the garden she is making at Kendal with plants associated with Quaker botanists.

favour of display. The exhibition is open from April to October, with occasional forays to other parts of the country during the winter.

Small travelling exhibitions of photographic reproductions are available all the year round, with a real panel if security is satisfactory. These are organised by Peter and Sheila Fox, who retired to Kendal to help with the tapestry. Both also steward regularly and Peter particularly enjoys demonstrating the embroidery techniques.

A new body, The Quaker Tapestry at Kendal, was set up and, for the first two years, its trustees employed two full-time staff, Chris Nash, a Penrith Friend with considerable management experience, and Bridget Guest, who moved to Kendal from Yorkshire, with expertise in teaching and running a shop. They started work before the building conversion was complete, and the dust had barely settled when the exhibition opened in April 1992.

After two years of incredibly hard work, Chris sadly had to leave and Bridget now runs the exhibition, with help from a part-timer, Sandra Lennon, and a dedicated band of volunteers, many of whom return year after year to steward.

Local volunteers include Joy Wallace, who steered through the legal agreement between the Quaker Tapestry Scheme and Kendal & Sedbergh monthly meeting, which owns the meeting house; Rachel Abbott, who moved to Kendal with her husband Ian to help with the tapestry; David Butler, who designed two of the panels and co-designed

another; and Robin Greaves, one of the two Friends who interviewed Anne Wynn-Wilson for Quaker Home Service when the tapestry was still an embryo growing out of a children's class.

Their work ranges from stewarding and serving in the shop to the back-room tasks of packing sale goods, addressing envelopes and pricing items for the shop. A quiet force in the background is Ann Cuming, who as well as cultivating the garden does a host of small but vital jobs, such as making cups of tea, fetching sandwiches, sitting quietly with visitors in the garden or ferrying Friends to and from the mainline station.

Many of the volunteers took part in the embroidery scheme, but by no means all. Some are overseas visitors who combine a holiday in the Lake District with stewarding work.

Tapestry workshops remain popular. These were originally taught by Anne Wynn-Wilson and Ann Nichols, who have now almost entirely handed over to Bridget Guest and Alison Burnley.

'There's nearly always a waiting list,' says Bridget. 'I take down enquirers' names and let them know when I can offer them a date.

'They are often people who want to learn Quaker stitch and we are getting an increasing number of embroiderers who are taking part in church millennium projects.'

She has now commissioned some new woollen embroidery fabric, made by Friends in Wales, which is both on sale and in use in the

*Sandra Lennon tucks the panels into their 'nighties' to
protect them from dust and light during the winter.*

demonstration area at the exhibition, where copies
are being made of some of the panels.

A popular feature of the exhibition is a video
area, where visitors rest on the old meeting house
benches and watch a recorded version of *Talking
threads*, stories from the Quaker Tapestry written
by Roy Apps and told by Barry Wilsher and Jill
Wilsher.

The live version of this, performed by Barry and
Jill, the two actors who started the *Quaker Peace
Action Caravan* depicted on panel B8, was first
shown at the Festival Hall exhibition and later
became a valued element of many tapestry
exhibitions.

Each year, a new small exhibition is mounted
alongside the main tapestry exhibition at Kendal.
These have included a series of embroidered
panels made by children from a school that visited

the exhibition, a quilt made by Elizabeth Morley
and Harrogate meeting, and embroidered panels
designed and made by Friends in Pickering & Hull
monthly meeting.

There is still a steady demand for talks and slide
shows and Bridget keeps a list of Friends across
the country who are able to present these.

While taking the whole exhibition out to other
venues is now a huge undertaking, it is hoped that
it will continue to be possible to do so from time to
time. Otherwise, the panels spend their winters
wrapped in their 'nighties', as Bridget calls them, to
protect them from light, dust and moth while she
and her volunteers, far from taking a well-earned
rest as might be imagined, prepare for the next
year's influx of visitors to view what an entry in the
visitors' book describes as 'Kendal's treasure, a
work of love'.

The Religious Society of Friends

Quakerism emerged from the religious and political ferment of the English civil war. One leader was George Fox, a young shoemaker from Leicestershire, whose disaffection with the religious forms of his time led him to travel the country seeking truth.

Eventually he found it in a vision which showed him that God could speak to everyone without priestly intervention. He taught that everyone had within them a divine witness. This was blasphemy in 1650 and he was soon imprisoned for preaching to the congregation of a church in Derby of 'the light within'.

His troubles with the law were just beginning. His pacifist convictions, his refusal to pay tithes to support a church and clergy that he had found wanting, his refusal to swear the oath of allegiance on the grounds that it implied double standards of truth and his insistence on preaching the message he had received all landed him in prison again and again.

As he travelled, he found many like-minded men and women. By the mid-1650s, Quakers (a nickname given by Justice Bennet, according to Fox's journal, 'as we bid them tremble at the word of the Lord') were becoming a significant movement.

Early Friends referred to themselves as Children of the Light or Friends of Truth. They met in silent, expectant worship, believing that the word may be given to any one of the worshippers, man, woman or child. Many travelled in the ministry to spread the word. Both men and women were frequently imprisoned, often simply for holding their meetings for worship as under the Conventicle Act any gathering of five or more adult dissenters 'under the colour or pretence of worship' was illegal.

A local and national structure soon became necessary to alleviate the suffering of those in prison (often far from home) and their families, to regulate the work of those who felt called to travel in the ministry and to press for changes in oppressive laws. Networks of local meetings were gathered into area monthly meetings, regional quarterly meetings, and a national yearly meeting – a structure which in Britain remains almost the same today. There are variations in other parts of the world.

All members of the society are entitled to take part in these 'meetings for worship for business' at each level.

In the early days, when much of the administrative business of the society concerned the sufferings of Friends for their faith, the national representative group charged with day-to-day business between the annual yearly meetings was known as Meeting for Sufferings, a name it still uses.

Monthly meetings still appoint elders and overseers to take special care of the right holding of meetings and the spiritual and pastoral welfare of Friends in each meeting. These appointments are short-term and unpaid.

Britain Yearly Meeting's corporate activities are administered from Friends House in Euston Road, London, which also houses a bookshop and library.

Groups of early Friends, like many other dissenters, settled in North America. Nineteenth-century emigration led to meetings in Australia, New Zealand and South Africa. These countries still have thriving Quaker meetings, as do many other parts of Africa, several European countries, the near East, India, Japan and Taiwan.

European, Australasian and some North American Friends still gather in silent worship, though significant numbers of Friends across the world have espoused programmed worship, often including hymns and using paid ministers.

Friends of all persuasions remain active in working for social and human rights issues across the world. Friends try to avoid taking jobs which might conflict with their commitment to justice, truth and the pacifist convictions most hold.

The absence of creed, clergy and sacraments does not mean the Religious Society of Friends has no structure or common core of belief. What it does mean is that no Friend is asked to affirm a belief not sincerely held and that a climate of openness prevails.

Membership of the Society implies acceptance of responsibility for keeping the meetings, for sharing the administrative and pastoral work and for bringing one's own life under the guidance of the Spirit.

Arrangement of panels

Panels were arranged in groups relating to a chapter or chapters in *Christian faith and practice* as approved by the Yearly Meeting of British Quakers in 1959. The titles of these chapters are given here, together with a list of panels in each group.

The title panel (The prism) was based on the preamble to chapter 1 (Spiritual experiences of Friends)

Section A (God and man) was based on the following chapters: 1 (Spiritual experiences of Friends), 2 (God and man), 3 (Friends and the Christian church):

A1 George Fox's convincement
A2 James Nayler
A3 James Parnell; Meeting for Sufferings
A4 Richard Seller
A5 Voyage of the *Woodhouse*
A6 John Woolman
A7 Conscientious objection
A8 Manchester Conference 1895
A9 Oaths

Section B (Publishing truth) was based on chapter 8 (Publishing truth):

B1 Firbank Fell: George Fox preaching
B2 Mary Fisher
B3 John Bright
B4 Publishers of Truth
B5 Stephen Grellet
B6 Woodbrooke
B7 Service overseas
B8 Quaker Peace Action Caravan

Section C (The meeting) was based on the following chapters: 4 (The meeting for worship), 5 (Vocal ministry), 6 (Retirement and prayer), 7 (The meeting as a fellowship), 15 (The world family of Friends):

C1 Swarthmoor Hall
C2 Margaret Fell
C3 Keeping the meeting
C4 Meeting houses
C5 Meeting houses overseas
C6 Meeting houses in the community
C7 Schools
C8 Marriage
C9 Pilgrimages
C10 Children and young people
C11 Leaveners

Section D (The art of living) was based on the following chapters: 9 (The art of living), 10 (Marriage and the home), 11 (Stages of life):

D1 George Fox: Lichfield, Pendle Hill
D2 Simplicity
D3 Persecution in Oxford
D4 Coalbrookdale
D5 Innocent trades
D6 Merchants
D7 Railways
D8 Botanists
D9 True health
D10 Scientists
D11 Industrial welfare
D12 Ecology
D13 Scott Bader Commonwealth

Section E (Social responsibilities) was based on chapter 12 (Social responsibilities):

E1 George Fox at Ulverston: healing
E2 John Bellers
E3 Bankering
E4 Criminal justice
E5 Elizabeth Fry
E6 Elizabeth Fry and the patchwork quilts
E7 Adult schools
E8 Ireland: The great hunger 1845-8
E9 Mary Hughes
E10 Unemployment
E11 Friends Provident Institution
E12 William Allen

Section F (National and international responsibilities) was based on the following chapters: 13 (National responsibilities), 14 (International responsibilities), 15 (The world family of Friends):

F1 George Fox in Derby gaol
F2 The Penn and Meade trial 1670
F3 The slave trade
F4 Daniel Wheeler
F5 Delegation to the Czar 1854
F6 Relief work: British Isles
F7 Relief work overseas
F8 Friends Ambulance Unit
F9 Northern Ireland: Reconciliation
F10 The Underground Railroad
F11 Penn and Pennsylvania
F12 Nantucket and Milford Haven
F13 Dolgellau and Pennsylvania
F14 New Zealand/Aotearoa
F15 Work camps
F16 Peace embassies
F17 Vigils for peace
F18 World Conference 1991
F19 South Africa
F20 Tasmania
F21 Canada
F22 The Netherlands 1940-5

The final panel (The world family of Friends) was based on chapter 15 (The world family of Friends)